Gerhard

Information Architecture
Basis and Future of CAAD

Birkhäuser – Publishers for Architecture
Basel • Boston • Berlin

Original manuscript in English

A CIP catalogue record for this book is available from the Library of Congress, Washington D.C., USA.

Deutsche Bibliothek Cataloging-in-Publication Data

Information architecture : basis of CAAD and its future / Gerhard Schmitt.
- Basel ; Boston ; Berlin : Birkhäuser, 1999
ISBN 3-7643-6092-5 (Basel ...)
ISBN 0-8176-6092-5 (Boston)

Original edition:
Information Architecture. Basi e futuro del CAAD (Universale di Architettura 43, collana diretta da Bruno Zevi; La Rivoluzione Informatica, sezione a cura di Antonino Saggio).
© 1998 Testo & Immagine, Turin

© 1999 Birkhäuser – Publishers for Architecture, P.O. Box 133, Ch-4010 Basel, Switzerland.
Printed on acid-free paper produced of chlorine-free pulp. TCF ∞
Printed in Italy
ISBN 3-7643-6092-5
ISNB 0-8176-6092-5

9 8 7 6 5 4 3 2 1

Contents

I am indebted to the many students and young colleagues whose design, teaching and research work appears in this book; in particular to Cristina Besomi, Bharat Dave, Maia Engeli, Fabio Gramazio, Urs Hirschberg, Rasmus Jörgensen, David Kurmann, Leandro Madrazo, Kuk Hwan Mieusset, Maria Papanikolaou, Werner Riniker, Mark Rosa, Patrick Sibenaler, Sibylla Spycher, Rudi Stouffs, Bige Tunçer, Eric van der Mark, Dieter von Buschmann, Daniel von Lucius, Andreas Weder and Florian Wenz. A special thanks to Malgorzata Miskiewicz-Bugajski for the layout and her input in the final stages.

Architecture and computers

Architecture – the word reminds us of buildings, gardens, and cities – the built environment. Computers – we associate the word with technology, precision, networks – the digital world. The term computer-aided architectural design (CAAD) connects the two worlds and points to the original idea behind using computers in architecture: to improve the built, physical environment by providing the best instruments and methods for the creators of architecture.

Drafting is not the main purpose of computers in architecture anymore. The computer is constantly changing its role and appearance, and becoming faster and more powerful in supporting designers every year. It was once useful to compare a computer to an electronic pencil or to a sophisticated typewriter. At the end of the twentieth century, this view would be a dangerous misconception of the machine, as it has moved into new areas of support. It can act as a medium, and in some cases already as a partner.

Architecture today consists of a complex process, a complex product, and a complex life cycle. In all phases, the computer is involved. In planning and designing, the machine helps to document, organize, and store information, to visualize design alternatives and to produce working drawings or models for the construction workers. The completed building – the product – is increasingly equipped with sensors, controllers, monitors and computers of all kinds. Once the building is in use, the computer is needed to support maintenance, calculate energy consumption and rent, monitor security and finally keep track of building parts for possible re-use.

This book will focus on the design of architecture and on the growing role of the computer in this process. There is a long and successful tradition of architects making use of new technology throughout the centuries. The advent of computers now offers design, construction, and management support that is by orders of magnitude better than all instruments before, but it also requires more complex knowledge. This book will give some insight into this new world.

Architecture and Information Technology

Architecture, at the cross-roads of arts and science for centuries, has always used information-processing devices (Oechslin 1993). Hardware, software and communication supported the builder and, later the architect, through the ages. This assumption, of course, is influenced by today's view of the world in terms of computers.

Nevertheless, there are strong relations between *hardware* and the ancient art of tool making and tool use in the form of measuring and drafting devices. *Software* can be related to the art and science of mathematics, which provided the builder and architect with the necessary instructions to apply the hardware. *Communication* is the art and necessity to receive, transform, translate, and store information and knowledge for further use.

The process of making architecture lends itself ideally to the application of abstract instruments and methods. From the time that the conception and making of architecture rested with the same person to the present situation of highly specialized persons cooperating to design and build architecture, there has been a steady shift from the material to the abstract aspects of architecture. Most of the value of buildings today no longer lies in its structural materials, but in the installations, in appliances, in communication and other equipment. More and more, even those material values are replaced by immaterial values, such as data bases and intelligent communication software as part of the building.

The relation between architecture and computing always ranged from enthusiastic acceptance to total rejection. The question of whether or not computing is just a tool or influences architecture directly has been a debate as emotional and as unresolved as the parallel discussion of whether architecture is an art or a science.

What differentiates today's situation from that of the past is our ability to externalize and describe the relation between computing and architecture more precisely. In the future, information will become a more important part of architecture, and special design knowledge will be needed to build information architecture.

What is CAAD?

Computer Aided Architectural Design describes a rapidly growing field in architectural practice, education and research. The better known generic term is CAD, Computer-Aided Design or Computer-Aided Drafting. Ivan Sutherland's thesis at the Massachusetts Institute of Technology (MIT) in 1963 is considered to be one of the fundamental starting points for CAAD (Sutherland 1963). In his dissertation he presented concepts that are still valid: interactivity, modular design, and object-oriented modeling. His work was central not only for architectural CAD systems, but for engineering in general. The book *Computer Aided Architectural Design* (Mitchell 1977) described the field's origins and state-of-the-art. The publication is still of value today in its main aspects. Both examples demonstrate that, in spite of a revolutionary technical development in the past two decades, the concepts and principles of CAAD have proven to be of long-term significance.

The commercial breakthrough for CAAD came in the early 1980s with the advent of the personal computer. Whereas sophisticated programs on mainframe and mini computers had existed for years, they were only affordable for the financially strongest architectural and engineering firms. As an example, Skidmore, Owings and Merril (SOM) in the United States produced their own software for several years and could achieve a vertical integration and presentation quality that PC programs accomplished only years later. The 1990s brought the general affordability of three-dimensional modeling, rendering, animation, and multimedia presentations, along with a concentration in the CAAD software industry. The significant development since the mid-1990s has been the growth of acceptance of the World Wide Web (WWW) and its applications.

Information as the fifth dimension of architecture

In 1946 Sigfried Giedion described time as the 4th dimension of architecture. Toward the end of the 20th century, information should be declared the 5th dimension of architecture. This information can be classified in four categories: (1) information residing in the designer's memory, directly influencing

ARCHITECTURE AND INFORMATION TECHNOLOGY

Crystallization of an information structure – the out view. Computer simulation by Malgorzata Miskiewicz-Bugajski, 1998.

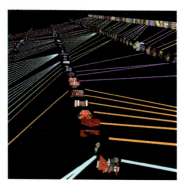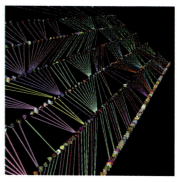

Using information technology to teach architecture: Individual designs and their work links are displayed on the Internet in the Phase(X)2 project (see Design teaching: Phase(X)2*). F. Gramazio, U. Hirschberg, P. Sibenaler, C. Besomi, B. Tunçer, 1998.*

Left: Core of information structure simulation, Malgorzata Miskiewicz-Bugajski, 1998. Right: Information and communication influencing architecture: Communication Center in Lausanne-Ecublens, Switzerland, completed in 1995. Architect Rodolphe Luscher, photo Aurelius Bernet.

the design, (2) information from outside, formalized external references, (3) information generated in the design and construction process itself, and (4) information coming into existence during the lifetime of the building.

Information in the designer's memory is the basis of architectural knowledge. It is supplemented with each new design process. Despite continuous attempts in the past, architectural knowledge is not understood and defined completely. The design methods movement took the first steps to formalize architectural information and to use it for the synthesis of buildings (Schmitt 1993, pp. 26-29). Presently, descriptive rather then prescriptive models of information for the design of buildings dominate in research.

The external information used in the design and construction process consists of building regulations and calculation methods, along with information about site and context. The formalized information describes patterns and agreements on the generally acknowledged conditions of buildings and physical laws that designers must know.

Designing and constructing a building creates new information. Besides the spatial and physical result, the design and building processes generate an information data base. The building in its entirety represents new information in the sense of collected data unified into a meaningful structure.

Data gathered during the physical existence of a building develops into the fourth class of information. It is becoming available only now that advanced sensory equipment and practically unlimited storage capacity of computers are available. This information is the foundation for new knowledge bases that will be used for the improvement of the second class of building information. In the long term, it becomes part of the immanent information in the designers' memory.

This classification of information and the combined use of it in design offers a bright future for architecture. As nature continues to develop through external factors, gradual selection and mutation, architecture will survive as a cultural value, transmitted and improved from generation to generation.

In post-industrial countries, the movement away from planning and building new objects towards an adaptive and re-use ori-

INFORMATION AS THE FIFTH DIMENSION OF ARCHITECTURE

Five dimensions of architecture in data space: the three spatial dimensions (xyz), time (the viewer can interactively travel through data space) and information that is mapped on and influences the other dimensions and the overall perception of data space. Florian Wenz, 1993.

ented process of thinking and building has begun. This will eventually improve the quality of built architecture. This development applies only to those countries with a stable or decreasing population. In countries with a rapidly increasing population, the problem of building and maintaining energy-efficient physical structures remains a major problem. Information technology can help to improve the situation through optimization and application of experiences from other countries. The computer as a medium that can store information will support this development. At the moment, the computer is mainly used to translate and improve existing ways of thinking, and to build faster and more efficiently. Its potential as an external knowledge base for architecture has not been recognized. The mine of information, accumulated in data bases, could be exploited and processed as a fifth dimension of architecture.

The computer as a communication tool
Information technology opens new communication possibilities by transporting data and information between different persons, between persons and machines, and between differ-

ent machines. IT therefore has the potential to augment and improve human communication. It could bridge the gap between individuals and computers by taking advantage of the machine's capabilities in processing and storing data. By strengthening human capabilities, IT could induce new discoveries and support creativity.

Information technology means for the information society what industry meant for the industrial society and what agriculture meant for the agricultural society. IT enables the creation of a world wide market of services and applications and facilitates collaboration in research, development and teaching.

In the information society, most of the institutions of the post-industrial era continue to exist as metaphors. The digital city, the data superhighway – an expression popularized by American Vice President Gore and President Clinton in the first half of the 1990s – as well as the firewalls to protect networks from unauthorized access, are just three examples. They are attempts to transform necessary institutions from one era to the next. History has taught us that this characterizes a time of transition after which entirely new structures and instruments will develop.

A critique of the information euphoria

Critique concerning the proliferation of information technology in the architectural office is common. The first type of criticism refers to the actual dangers resulting from depending on vast networks that are difficult to control. Individuals in architectural and engineering offices are concerned that they have no control over the data and cannot trace the whereabouts and accumulation of personal information. They question the reliability of seemingly secure communication channels.

An early example is the crash of a part of the American AT&T telephone network in 1990, when more than 60,000 people lost their service and more than 70 million phone calls could not be completed.

The second type of criticism is more philosophical. It sometimes occurs that former enthusiasts reverse their opinion to condemnation when their hopes and expectations are not fulfilled.

More serious is the critique by specialists in the field. Clifford Stoll is one of them. In his book *Die Wüste Internet*, he claims that

> little information in the World Wide Web is really useable. During business hours, the network is painfully slow and more costly than other means of communication. Computer networks isolate people from each other and remove them from reality, they undermine education and creativity by questioning the roles of schools and libraries... The Internet community has turned into a self-sufficient community since the early 1990s without a sense for overall responsibility. Their texts are mediocre, frail in content and are weak communication nonsense. The term interactive media network means nothing, yet simulates intimacy. (Stoll 1995).

Much of the criticism relates to problems connected with technical aspects of information technology that will disappear as the field matures. The toughest and most serious critique is that directed at the *Leitbild* or model of IT as an instrument that replaces human labor and human jobs. This critique will remain with us until we provide the computer with its appropriate role in society – which will be quite different from today's view.

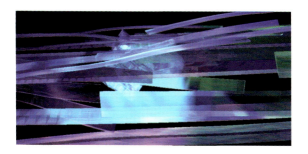

Information structure simulation - connectors. Malgorzata Miskiewicz-Bugajski, 1998.

The computer as a new instrument in the architectural office

Architecture and its instruments share a rich history, as Werner Oechslin points out in his essay *Computus et Historia* (Oechslin 1993). In antiquity, those tools were measuring devices and philosophical theories with instrumental character. Today, they are technically advanced physical instruments – such as machines and robots – and intellectual instruments – such as smart software.

The computer as a tool or instrument has been most successful in terms of efficiency. One reason is that a clear paradigm or *Leitbild* exists for this purpose. Yet the definition of the computer as a mere tool does not take into account that it not only emulates office instruments, but also simulates new design instruments, unthinkable without the computer. These instruments can turn into self-generating and self-referential systems.

Many architects, alarmed by the emergence of the new computing environment, found solace in the hope that the computer would be just another instrument. But this view of a computer can correspond to a regressive *Leitbild*. A computer tool under such a paradigm must prove itself in eliminating previously human activities with less cost and higher quality. While this might be a goal for short term gains, it is a dangerous development in the long term. If one considers the computer as an instrument only, it must pay for itself in that it perfectly replaces activities that were previously difficult or boring or expensive to achieve.

Examples are word processors, when seen as replacing typists; spreadsheets, when seen as replacing calculators; CAD programs, when seen as electronic pencils; office automation programs, when seen as a collection of desktop activities; rendering programs, when only seen as a way to impress clients. Those instruments pose the problem that they directly aim at eliminating expensive human labor. Even more questionable from an intellectual standpoint is the assumption that human skills are directly transported to the computer, which in turn is then "personalized" or "humanized."

The computer becomes the repository of activities that were once human. Because machines cannot yet reason about, improve or question their own abilities, it also implies that these transferred activities are then frozen in their present state. With this, the computer could become a retarding, regressive instrument that hinders progress.

One could argue that the elimination of those human activities will result in the creation of new information processing jobs, as the development in the United States in the 1990s demonstrates. In addition, computer tools provide us with a yet unknown freedom to explore complexity and relations within structures. New and old techniques are confronted, assigning a new position and possibilities to old techniques or eliminating them.

The Internet as an information source for architects

The Internet is a network of networks, connecting more than 60 million people in 1997. The data transfer volume between connected computers has multiplied since 1991, when only a few thousand participants, mainly in universities, were on-line.With its networked information storage, the Internet forms the new infrastructure for the information age. In the Internet, the equivalent of today's streets, trains and airports are cables and satellite connections; the equivalent of today's retail stores and production places are the individual information servers connected to networked workstations.

Before the introduction of the World Wide Web, the Internet already existed, but it was more difficult to use for the computer illiterate. The file transfer protocol (FTP) allowed the sending of files, Telnet allowed the log-on to another machine, the gopher program based on FTP and Telnet was a step toward the simplification of search and data exchange. But only the introduction of the first browser based on the HTML (Hyper Text Markup Language) standard brought wide acceptance of the Internet and allowed the combination of all protocols in one shell.

Today the Internet combines the advantages of mainly shallow information, existing libraries, compact discs and on-line information. Disadvantages – such as getting lost in the incredible

THE COMPUTER IN THE ARCHITECTURE OFFICE

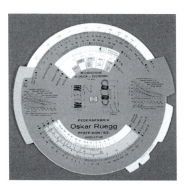

Facing page: Simulation of the new design for the ETH Zürich Scientific Visualization Center (VISDOME). Patrick Siebenaler, 1998. Above left: Engineering instrument. A slide rule for measuring springs. Federfabrik Pfäffikon, Switzerland. Photo Aurelius Bernet. Right: Architecture and engineering instrument. Drawing table, Sauter Bachmann AG Zahnräderfabrik, Netstal, Switzerland. Below: Information Structure - Gate one, Malgorzata Miskiewicz-Bugajski, 1998.

amount of information – are known, but they are reduced by improved search robots and new ways to better structure information.

Architects and the construction industry are beginning to use the Internet. They see it first as a source for documentation, but increasingly also as a source for services. The development started in the United States with the appearance of a few architectural office descriptions placed on the homepage of the American Institute of Architects (Sanders 1996). In Switzerland, the CRB (Centre Suisse d'Etudes pour la Rationalisation de la Construction) began in 1997 with the establishment of *OpusLine*, which will eventually give its members access to the Internet and secure communication between subscribers. The youth organization of the SIA (Schweizerischer Ingenieur und Architektenverband, [http://www.sia.ch]) went on-line the same year [http://www.junge-sia.ch/]. Individual architects and groups of offices are advertising their capabilities on the Internet [http://www.work-shop-archiV.de].

Data Bases - Building Memories

Data bases and data base systems are schemata for organizing data (Korth 1991). As they can store and access a multitude of complex information, they become crucial in the construction, documentation, and facility management phase.

The best-known data base systems are hierarchical, network, relational and object oriented systems. Relational data bases are the most common today. Typical applications are business and administration, bookkeeping and personnel data management. Object-oriented data bases offer the capability of designing and maintaining complex and flexible data models. Entries into this type of data base are objects with their own data structure and their own data-access methods. They can easily describe technical systems and are therefore interesting for building management.

A data base is installed on one computer or on several computers in a network. Distributed data bases allow storage of data in the place where they originate or in the place where they are needed most frequently. This leads to the optimization of data transfer and access time. Project data bases in architecture can act as the building's memory and have constant access to life data and enable complex data queries (von Buschmann 1995). The use of data for facility management will become easier, and all necessary data for remodeling a building is already accessible. During the lifetime of a building, data concerning the temperature, lighting conditions, electricity and energy consumption can automatically be traced and entered into the data base. This data can then be turned into information necessary to optimally maintain and control the building.

The long term goal of such a system is to create a knowledge base for architectural design, based on a multitude of data from different structures. Building data can be entered automatically into a *Black Box* (a metaphor from the airline industry), a device that accompanies a building from its conception throughout its life time. This data base can be used for data mining and result in important new findings about architecture. Thus, the memory of a single building and the collective memory of many buildings can develop into an important source for new design.

Drawing and Modeling

Each phase of the design process favors the application of a particular drawing and modeling medium. Education – before and during university – focuses more on conventional drawing and modeling methods than on computer methods. If one considers the purpose of a sketch, to quickly record a thought and to communicate it to others, the combination of paper and pen will be irreplaceable for a while. If the task is to draw or sketch a building from memory, the advantages of paper are less clear. If the task is the exact documentation during the design phase, the advantages of computer-based drawing and modeling become obvious. The benefits are the computer's capability of structuring, storing, automating and manipulating.

The existing computer sketching and paint programs are no threat to conventional drawing because they mostly imitate conventional media. But the next generation of drawing and modeling programs could demonstrate the advantages of the

INTERNET AND ARCHITECTURE

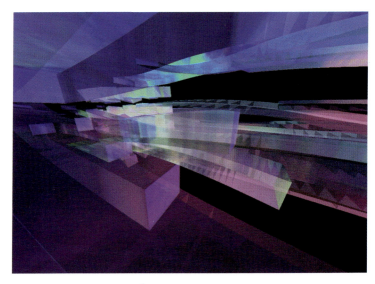

Above: AltaVista search refinement module – Architecture. It allows for research in user-defined hierarchical structures. Below: Information structure simulation – pulsating data channels. Malgorzata Miskiewicz-Bugajski, 1998.

computer: they will support the structuring of the design process, they will facilitate the storage of different versions, they will automate repetitive tasks and they will simplify the revision of drawings.

A model describes reality at different levels of abstraction. To understand these levels, the qualities of the individual abstractions need to be known. Some aspects relate to both physical and digital modeling. During the entire time of modeling, a dialog between the designer and the model occurs. In physical modeling, this is a permanent process, whereas in digital modeling it is a cycle of model building and model evaluation.

The model is a much-needed support for spatially complex design because such complex compositions can hardly be recognized in their entirety with other means. The spatial arrangement and complexity of the design is recognized only at the moment of modeling. The model becomes a design instrument, because most of the qualities of the design can be evaluated in the model. In physical modeling, the tactile treatment of materials and the placing of elements is dominant.

Digital models present a new situation in that they are used mainly for visualization and evaluation and in that the interaction with the digital modeler as a design tool does not yet occur frequently (McCullough 1997). A short-term goal is for the design process using digital models to take place in parallel with physical modeling. As digital modeling is directly related to the quality of the modeling program, it will become more powerful over time.

In digital modeling, a clear abstraction is necessary to assign the correct information content to each representation. The possible information depth of a digital model is rarely used today. In most cases, the digital model is derived from traditional methods which are then simulated with digital means. For example, the level of detail in a digital model can vary without destroying the character and the essence of the model. Quite the opposite: the information content of such a model increases, because it only details those areas that are of interest for a specific reason. This change in information depth in a structure can not occur in physical models, and therefore it

DATA BASES - BUILDING MEMORIES

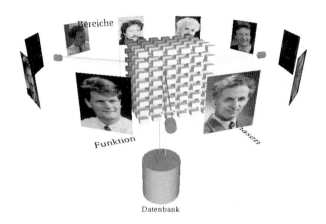

Above: Visual description of a building data base. Project partners cooperate through a common cube interface as a navigation interface for activities, phases and functions. The cube also serves as interface for the data base, shown at the bottom of the image. Paul Meyer and Dieter von Buschmann, 1996. Below: The metaphor of space as interface to a data base. Clicking on the images provides access to additional information spaces. Monika Isler, 1996.

represents a clear advantage of the digital model. The numerical input of objects, scale and proportions is hindering the progress of free modeling. Programs such as *Sculptor* (see *Design instrumentarium: Sculptor*) attempt to eliminate this disadvantage.

Direct interaction with the complete virtual model is fundamental for the future design process (see *Virtual Reality*). Today, data structure, representation and interface restrictions are the most serious hindrances to reaching this goal. Partial and isolated solutions are available, so it is necessary to use other instruments at each design stage. Although the use of different digital modeling instruments will lead to information loss between applications, it will be necessary for the foreseeable future (Streich 1996).

Simulation

Simulation is the representation of an object based on an appropriate abstraction and a model. Simulation techniques help us to understand designs and buildings better. Simulation has a long history, starting with wood, stone, clay and paper models as examples.

In Switzerland, travelers are often astonished when seeing strange objects in fields, in cities, or attached to buildings. These are so-called *Baugespanne* or outlines of buildings in a scale of 1:1. They simulate the new building in its actual situation and size. Their purpose is to visualize the planned building volume before it is actually built and to enable people who live close to the planned building to voice their concerns. The Kröller-Müller house project from 1912 by Mies van der Rohe, for which a 1:1 scale wood and fabric model was built, is an example for this type of building simulation. A more recent example is the reconstruction of parts of the Berlin castle which was demolished after the Second World War. This 1:1 simulation, constructed of metal scaffolding and printed fabric, intended to recreate the original image of the Berlin castle as realistically as possible.

Computer simulations are a new way to predict how a planned building or object may look and how it can be experienced in space and time. The digital integration of an object

DRAWING AND MODELING

Conceptual 2D Photoshop sketches for a Music and Art Center in Jyväskylä, Finland. CAAD praxis course, ETH Zürich. Malgorzata Miskiewicz-Bugajski, 1997.

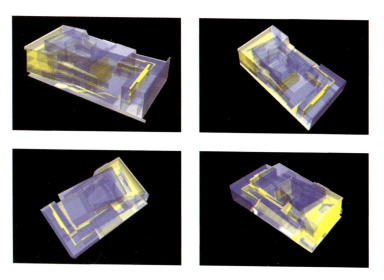

Volumetric study of space differentiation using transparency maps. Music and Art Center in Jyväskylä, Finland. CAAD praxis course ETH Zürich. Form°Z modeling, Malgorzata Miskiewicz-Bugajski, 1997.

in its environment is necessary so that its scale and relation to the existing architecture can be experienced. For quick visualizations, it is sufficient to choose a photograph or a video as context representation. While this technique appears attractive, the traditional representation of context in the form of sketches required the client to abstract, and thus gave the architect the opportunity to present the design idea more clearly. In addition, photographs often show unimportant objects, such as cable, signals, and posts, so that the new design might react inappropriately to these disturbances.

Virtual Reality
The appearance of the first architectural drawing started a development for which the next and logical step was the development of virtual reality. But already dating back to the 10th century, architectural drawings in Europe were the first kind of abstractions that appeared *virtually real* to potential clients and builders – real enough to base decisions on. With the dis-

26

Paper sketches and their equivalent on the computer. Because exploratory digital models can be used in the design process, they should not be considered as being final products. Oscar Guijar, 1995.

covery of perspective techniques, drawings became more refined and developed into a form of art with numerous branches, ranging from technical drawings to presentation drawings. Wooden models appeared even before the Renaissance and were supplemented in the nineteenth century with paper and cardboard models. Each new invention helped to improve the understanding of architectural projects by reducing abstraction while increasing the complexity of the representation (Schmitt 1993, Schmitt et al. 1995).

Architectural VR is based on a model of physical reality that is stored in the computer as an interactive data set and related operations. Through an interface, the designer or client accesses aspects of reality represented in the model which affect different human senses. The technique is known as simulation (see *Simulation*) and can be used to explore the geometry, as well as the cost, the structural stability or the energy behavior of a building. VR enables the interactive exploration of these models and to the acquisition of a wealth of new impressions or insights that were filtered out by traditional abstractions. Because simulation is a precursor to VR, the transition between simulation and VR is fluid. Whereas simulations are at the core of VR, VR is not needed for all simulations. The two most critical aspects of VR, interaction and immersion, facilitate the direct manipulation of objects and the feeling of being inside the simulated space. Head mounted displays seem to be the natural choice as the enabling devices. However, the lack of display quality and other restrictions of head mounted displays make large-size stereo projection more attractive. This allows the simultaneous access to virtual models for many people.

Architects first intensely criticized the new technology, before adopting and improving it with domain specific contributions. The knowledge of architectural abstraction and simulation is useful to the further development of VR and vice versa. Today, the newest methodological and technical instruments help designers create a more responsible architecture, many aspects of which can be experienced and tested before construction. This includes the possibility of expanding the number of senses addressed for the explanation of an architectural idea.

Virtual reality is a new simulation technique that is gaining acceptance also in medicine, mechanical engineering, chemistry, economics, archaeology and many other disciplines. In architecture, the acceptance of this technique is growing slowly, because the needed computing power and the necessary know-how to produce convincing VR presentations are still very expensive. With faster and less expensive computers, VR becomes a realistic additional possibility of presentation in architectural practice even for small projects.

Architecture as a discipline between science and art has developed the ability to communicate powerful ideas with extremely abstract means of presentation. Since the beginnings of Modern Architecture, these abstractions have begun to influence design itself and the creation of new form (Madrazo 1995, Madrazo 1996). Design abstractions become the basis for future architecture, while the previously built architectural

SIMULATION

 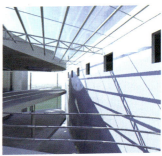

Top: Photorealistic Radiance rendering of the Jyväskylä Music and Arts Centre auditorium entrance at 14:00 and 16:00 on June 21. Comparing results from Radiance (right) and Lightscape (left). Dorota Palubicka, 1997.

Simulating artificial light. Interior renderings of the Jyväskylä Music and Arts Centre concert hall for two different stage and lighting settings. Dorota Palubicka, 1997.

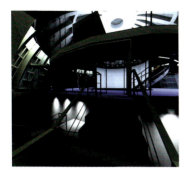 

Artificial lighting as a design element. Radiance rendering of the proposed virtual reality center in the central dome of the ETH Zürich. Model and simulation Patrick Sibenaler, 1998. Left: access to the dome and curved projection wall. Right: the lower gallery with the entrance.

reality turns into an abstraction of the past. Thus, with the dissolving boundary between reality and abstraction, and the tendency of architecture to move away from the craft of building towards the art of creating virtual structures, VR becomes the perfect vehicle to simulate new architecture. This could eventually result in the de-materialization of architecture.

Architecture is a natural application area for VR. Each plan, each perspective attempts to provoke an illusion in the observer's mind which, through a minimum of means, achieves a maximum impact. A visually trained person is able to perfectly understand a hand sketch consisting of only a few lines which communicate a proposed building, the architect's personal design language, and much more. Laymen, however, are often not able to judge the quality of an architectural proposal based on two- and three-dimensional abstractions only. They are even less able to evaluate the relations between the form, function, behavior and cost of a proposed design. A virtual model with a high degree of detail which covers all of these aspects in an integrated manner, and which designers and clients can explore in any way, will therefore be of significant help.

The introduction of computer-aided architectural design (CAAD) has demonstrated that the geometric-graphical presentation of an object is only one, although important, abstraction. VR confirms the fact that reducing a computer to an electronic pencil is a dead end, because this only facilitates faster ways of producing the mistakes of the past. An appropriate model for a building must be found, which is more than the sum of its parts (see *Design Teaching: Phase(X)*).

The new possibilities of VR increase the need for a meaningful and integrated representation for the simulation of architecture – from design through construction and facility management, which includes all stages of a building's life after it has been completed.

CSCW: a new kind of team work

Computer-supported collaborative work (CSCW) offers the possibility of working together in spite of being separated spatially. Computer-supported collaborative design (CSCD) is a special kind of CSCW, a fast-growing area in information technology. Working together in an electronically linked team is a most attractive addition to working individually. It can foster synergies and lead towards a goal much faster, because the combined knowledge of the partners often leads to a breakthrough. Teams are forming spontaneously, if spatial distances exist and if the people interested in collaborating have flexible working conditions. If this is not the case, the collaborative work must be agreed on in advance.

CSCW is possible only in networked computer environments. Computers can be connected in a local area network (LAN) or in a spatially distributed wide area network (WAN). The largest network is the Internet, through which worldwide distributed partners can organize collaboration. Communication over the Internet is standard in scientific computing today and is gaining ground in engineering and architectural firms that operate internationally or with remote partners.

CSCW supports different types of communication each of which has specific technical prerequisites. Depending on the task and on how many people are cooperating, a CSCW environment needs e-mail, video, audio, a common drawing platform (whiteboard), direct written communication (talk), file transfer, and the shared use of programs (application sharing). The combined use of these different instruments defines the main difference to the video telephone or picture telephone, that has been known since the 1930s.

Video contact is essential for communication through the network. To achieve good quality even with low bandwidth, several techniques are used to compress the image on the side of the sender and decompress it on the side of the receiver. The resolution is kept low and only those parts of the image that change are transmitted. To be able to send audible information through the same line and at the same time as visual information, the sound also needs to be compressed. Temporary interruptions of audio or video transmission can be compensated briefly by the other medium.

The whiteboard allows users to sketch directly or to comment on the work of others. The talk window is useful for quickly transmitting written information, especially for establishing audio or video connections (see *The Virtual Design Studio (VDS): Multiplying Time*).

The exchange of data and files during a CSCW session is essential. For this, programs exist that are based on the file transfer protocol (FTP). FTP is being increasingly superseded by direct exchange through more user friendly Internet applications. It is also possible to take remote control of another computer from one's own machine to simplify work on the same project. With full remote control over another computer in a different place, it is possible to leave delicate configuration, design or change operations to the most experienced person in the team.

By the end of the 20th century, CSCW has been established as a possible form of education. Early experiments of CSCW in education date back to 1994, when virtual design studios between MIT and European and Asian universities were implemented. Teaching is an ideal test field for the further development of CSCW because during those experiments students and programmers can learn at the same time.

Typical applications are the transmission of lectures and exercises, enabling communication between students and professors; the follow-up on experiments or the examination of models in distant laboratories; collaborative work on design problems; and, finally, the presentation and critique of a pro-

Radiance simulation of the interior of the Gessnerallee Theater in Zürich. The result was printed in the highest possible resolution on large fabric sheets and mounted on the facade of the theater as scaffolding protection. This way, prospective visitors could have a look at the future – and therefore virtual – interior while it was being built. Urs Hirschberg, 1996.

Left: VR and Augmented reality. Maia Engeli and David Kurmann interacting with a virtual model that is projected in stereo on the 3x6 meter screen of the Architectural Space Laboratory (ASL) at ETH Zürich. Note that they can see and interact with each other at the same time. Right: David Kurmann rotating a cube in a virtual sculptor model in the ASL, an environment suited for designing spaces from the inside out in 1:1 scale.

ject through the network. For successful use of CSCW in teaching, it is important that a differential of information exists between the parties involved. Cooperation is not something that simply happens, but it occurs when there is a true desire to learn from somebody or to give information to somebody. This information differential – and curiosity – fosters collaboration from the beginning.

The Virtual Design Studio (VDS): Multiplying Time

With increasing globalization and specialization in the design 36 and building industry, collaboration between partners in remote locations becomes crucial. Ideally, all of them could work on a building design at any place, simultaneously together (synchronously) or separately (asynchronously), while the latest state of the design would always be available to all team members.

There would be collaborative work on a common object and no information lost in transfer of files. Such a system does not exist yet for the architectural domain, but similar programs are available for simpler applications: shared data bases or shared calendar and address files, through which several people organize their appointments and contacts.

The *Multiplying time* project comes close to this goal. It allows the continuous work on a design or a set of designs through different time zones around the world at the same time. The task was to design a house for a painter and a writer on an island west of Seattle, USA. The project developed in several phases.

As a first step, three partners from ETH Zürich, the University of Hong Kong, and the University of Seattle agreed on a common project. They formulated the design brief, using e-mail and personal meetings. It was decided that students should work for one week on the design in three different time zones, thus multiplying one week into three work weeks. The interactive program *Sculptor* by David Kurmann was installed in all three locations to enable synchronous and asynchronous design. Data exchange was enabled with a data base directly connected to the Internet, similar to that of *Phase(X)* (see *Design teaching: Phase(X)*).

On the morning of the first day, students in Hong Kong started with the design. At the end of their 8-hour working day, they deposited the results in the common data base that could be seen by all partners through the browser interface. Students from Zürich began 8 hours later and could thus base their decisions on the results achieved by their Hong Kong partners. They also placed their designs in the common data base, so that students from Seattle were able to explore the designs from Zürich and Hong Kong by the time they started to work. In addition, video conferences took place every 8 hours, during which students could share and explain their ideas. The setup thus created an intense global think-tank, operating 24 hours a day.

Every day, a new phase was introduced along with a new design issue. In each phase, students could select a design to develop further from any of the three locations. On the last day, a video conference between all three locations took place for the evaluation of the final design proposals. Authors and critics discussed the individual designs and observed the design threads. Students from the three locations noticed that, although they had not known each other before, they found a common language to communicate. The basis for this language were the modeling program and the individual designs.

In a follow-up to this experiment, a group of students at the Technical University of Delft continued where the previous exercise had ended. The Delft students used a different set of software, but had access to all stages of the previous design phases through the data base. In three additional phases, they developed more refined solutions.

The *Multiplying time* experiment demonstrated that it is possible to work from a common data base, taking advantage of different time zones and special capabilities of particular sites: Seattle provided the site, Hong Kong the first design models, Zürich the modeling program, Delft special rendering techniques.

The resulting designs are of shared authorship, but the individual contributions are clearly identifiable, along with the evolvement of the design. The complete results can be found at [http://space.arch.ethz.ch/VDS_97/].

Engineering Data Management Systems (EDMS)

Engineering Design Management Systems (EDMS) are a special type of computer-supported collaborative work environment. An EDMS allows the cooperation between different partners in the design process under highly regulated but secure conditions. It is implemented on one server with the data base and several clients or in distributed data base systems. Files, such as text, images or CAD files are stored together with their meta-information. This meta-information reports on the owner of the file, the access rights, the time of creation and modification, as well as other attributes that can be specified for each project and each partner. Using meta-data, files can be classified based on different criteria. Other features are versioning and workflow management. An EDMS can be installed or accessed on a large number of computers in a local or global network to enable collaboration on a project.

Facility Management

Moving into a new building initiates a process that has the largest impact on the overall cost of a building: considering all expenses associated with a structure, including salaries, energy and maintenance expenditures, the original costs of construction are usually less than 10% of the entire sum.

The first years already bring renovations and remodelings as a reaction to changed requirements of the clients or changing conditions.

Facility management (FM) includes a multitude of services, which so far occurred mostly uncoordinated and in different places. The communication equipment, the electrical system, heating and ventilating, water and sewage must be maintained and renovated constantly. The building cleaning must function flawlessly, rooms must be renovated, the exterior needs maintenance, in winter snow removal may be necessary. Dislocations of people or departments within a building must occur without interruption of the workflow. Next to these known activities, facility management has the purpose of improving the quality of working conditions. Ergonomy of the work place, appropriate choice of materials, and opti-

MULTIPLYING TIME

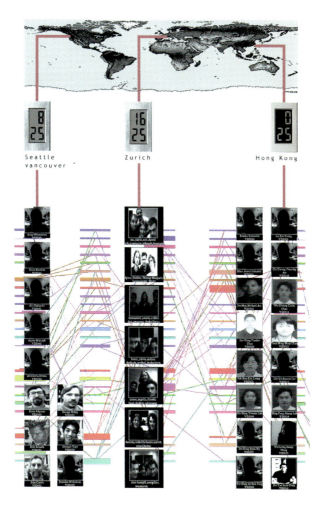

Facing page: Snapshots from the Multiplying Time *studio. The images show the development from conceptual models (top) to more refined projects (bottom) that developed in 5 days in three time zones. Top: Phase1* Dualities, *by S. Margaris, S.Lemmerzah, T. Musy - ETH Zürich; Phase 3* Light & Shadow, *by Siu Hong Ryan and Chi Kit Benson - Hong Kong. Bottom: Phase 8* Situation, *A. Amin, P. de Ruiter - Delft. Collected by Malgorzata Miskiewicz-Bugajski, 1998.*
Above: The Multiplying Time *setup and participants. The individual designs of the first phases are shown underneath with the connections between the student projects. Malgorzata Miskiewicz-Bugajski, 1998.*

38

mization of the lighting situation are just a few of the tasks to be resolved.

Facility management is a chance and a challenge for architects. It is a chance, because it opens new job opportunities and allows the improvement of the building even after it has been completed. It is a challenge because if forces architects and other partners in the planning and design process to consider factors that do not belong to the traditional area of expertise of architects. Facility management is a growing field in education, whose students are organized in the international facility management association (IFMA). This so far very practice-ori-

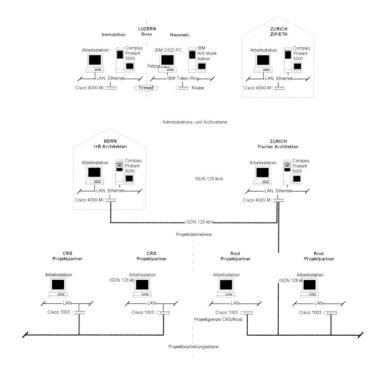

Schema of an EDMS in operation. The archive server of the client (top left) and consultant (top right), the project architects (middle) and the project partners (bottom) are connected with ISDN lines that also link to the computers on the construction site. Marcel Braungardt, 1997.

ented research has started at CIFE, the Center of Integrated Facility Engineering of Stanford University [http://www-leland. stanford.edu/group/CIFE], at VTT, the technical research center of Finland [http://www.vtt.fi/] and in the engineering department at ETH Zürich. Facility management is unthinkable without computers. Appropriate programs have appeared on the market, mostly as additions to CAD and data base programs.

A critique of the computerization of the architectural office

The criticism of the computerization of the architectural office was less eminent than the criticism concerning the computerization of the core area of architecture – the design process.The chance to shorten design time and improve communication comes at a cost. Office owners realized that it could take over assignments in administration, writing and calculation that were formerly handled by secretaries. The reason was the increasing accessibility of text processing and other office automation programs and the increased workflow pace. Architects faced the almost unsolvable task of supplementing or replacing paper storage with computer-based storage that required a new organization and discipline. In spite of the associated much lower costs of computer data storage – cheaper than paper storage by a factor of two to five – the additional effort of maintaining paper and computer storage could increase the overall cost of storage.

The legal implications of automating document handling and office automation are still not entirely solved. Frequently asked critical questions are: who is responsible when transmission and exchange problems occur that have consequences for the entire building? Who guarantees the security and protection from unauthorized data manipulation? The rapidly changing versions of programs and the fact that hardware is obsolete as soon as it enters the office require a high degree of patience and stamina. It is a question of perspective whether one observes these facts as problems or challenges.

More serious is the criticism regarding the changing role of the human in the office. From the beginning, computerization has led to an increased separation of work even in small offices. The office partners concentrate as before on acquisition and design, but the so-called CAD operators are gradually replacing the draftpersons. As the partners were lacking technical understanding of the new tool, they could not use the machine themselves and often did not realize the unused potential, in spite of the large financial investment. The CAD operators, on the other hand, were and are over-stressed motorically and under-stressed mentally.

CAAD in design: the computer as a medium

A medium is more than a tool or a method. It is an interactive counterpart, not necessarily an intelligent being, but something that has knowledge and capabilities to offer in the area we are interested in. A computer-aided architectural design environment, equipped with the necessary components and in cooperation with a competent designer, can achieve the status of a design medium. In this case, the architectural discourse can rise to the level of a medium that will not take away work, but that will allow design partners to deal with fundamental questions of future architecture more competently (Schmitt 1997).

Architectural design is more than playful interaction with geometric forms, supported by increasingly more attractive computer tools. Architecture today does not suffer from too much technology, but from the inappropriate application of the technology. It should not be the paradigm for CAAD to design the most complex artifacts of civilization with drafting programs simulating the computer as an electronic pencil only. Instead, architects should take advantage of simulation and communication technology on the best possible level during the design process.

Missing experience in realizing and controlling certain actions and relations in the building process is no excuse for retreating to a position of decorating rather than designing. If architects want to keep and improve their role in the building process in the future, they need to employ the computer more effectively. This could include its use as a design support medium that assists designers in areas where they do not have sufficient knowledge or competence themselves. The most obvious application for the computer as a medium is interactive simulation. More advanced applications are computer supported methods and agents (Schmitt 1996b). Research and education in architecture should place more emphasis on introducing the computer as a medium with various capabilities in order to improve the chances of architecture graduates in the long term.

The Building as an Information System

There are at least three stages during which a building can show an analogy to a system. The first stage includes the planning, design and construction of the building. The site and the context are entered in the data base, or they are read from existing data sets. The planning and design team works in a collaborative design environment (see *Computer-supported Collaborative Design - a new kind of team work*). They access the common model with an Internet browser, the data sets residing either in a common data base or with the individual design and planning partners who are organized as a virtual firm. The common model is also used during construction so that it can be based on an up-to-date representation of the entire design. When the building is completed, the collected data of the first stage is entered into the *Black Box* (see *Data Bases - Building Memories*).

The second stage represents the building until its physical end. During this building life cycle, all changes and performance data must be collected and entered into the *Black Box*, so that they can be used for the optimal maintenance and facility management of the building. Sensors can collect data automatically and feed them into the *Black Box* as well. The building representation would give a close image of the actual performance and behavior of the building so that it can be monitored constantly. In this stage, the building comes closest to performing as a system. With appropriate software, self-regulation of the building is possible.

The third stage represents the building as a case base for future data and information mining. Case studies of buildings could be used for data and information mining. This way, new findings about the behavior of buildings could be based on real data for the first time and could be reused in the design project. Similar to the proliferation of memes in the design studio (see *Design Teaching: Phase(X)*), good qualities would spread in the design process, whereas unsuccessful features would disappear over time in analogy to a natural selection.

Design Methods: Prototypes

Prototypes are conceptional schemata for the representation of generalized design knowledge. Design with prototypes implies generating a variation of an existing prototype that fulfills the requirements of the design. Operations with prototypes fall into three classes: prototype refinement, prototype adaptation, and prototype creation. This classification maps directly to applications in routine, innovative, and creative design (Gero and Maher 1993).

Prototype refinement is the best-understood and most-used method to produce variations of a prototype. The final product is created by adjusting the variables of the prototype without changing its fundamental structure. Prototype adaptation attempts to apply an existing design solution with few modifications to a new design problem. This means the modification of a prototype through the modification of variables, design elements, and design operations. Prototype creation is the most difficult task and corresponds to a completely new design.

In architecture, certain building types, materials or configurations prove their value over time. The essential of such an object, be it a piece of furniture or a building, can be described as a prototype. In each era, one of those prototypes has its meaning and, without much mental effort, a number of acceptable solutions can be generated by adjusting a prototype to a new situation.

Working with prototypes is much more concrete than the top-down or bottom-up methods which can also be applied to design, but it is more restricted in its results. It is possible to work with prototypes at different levels of abstraction. The

One view of the TRACE OutWorld. Florian Wenz and Fabio Gramazio, 1996.

adaptation of a prototype on the level of building functions can have more architectural impact than changes applied on the geometric abstraction level. This implies that a building prototype, for example in the form of a diagram, is as adaptable as a geometric prototype.

In contrast to the top-down or bottom-up methods, working with a prototype necessitates the understanding and the manipulation of an entire object whose parts have clear relations among each other internally and which is defined as a whole.

Design Methods: Case-Based Reasoning

Case-based reasoning (CBR) is the attempt to simulate a real object or the memory of experts in its entirety and uncompiled. This differentiates CBR from other knowledge-based systems that compile expert knowledge in the form of rules beforehand. Case-based reasoning uses the act of remembering to discover similar solutions in the past (Schank 1982). Applications of this research area, in existence since the early 1980s, reach from planning (Hammond 1989) to military applications to architecture (Schmitt and Dave 1996). A case-based system solves new problems by first searching for the most closely related case and by then adapting this case to the new situation. For this reason, cases must be indexed according to different aspects. If an adaptation from a single case is not possible, the system combines and adapts partial problem solutions from several cases. This avoids the multiple solution of similar problems as well as difficulties in the formulation of general rules and their modification for special cases. Case-based reasoning thus offers the opportunity to improve human learning and memory capabilities with the computer.

Case-based reasoning is a method that has been known in architecture for a long time. It consists of comparing a new situation to existing situations, selecting appropriate architectural solutions and adapting those solutions. The motivation for such an approach is simple: good experiences from the past should be kept, and mistakes that were made should not be repeated. Main problems are the completeness of case-based methods for finding appropriate cases and the adaptation of cases to the new requirements in geometric as well as in topological aspects. The largest and most complete case base is the built environment as a basis for all new design. A first step of abstraction are the works of architectural history, that describe crucial, but not all aspects of a building.

At the beginning of architectural studies, the case base of students consists only of the direct experiences of surrounding architecture. During education, the number of known cases grows continuously. Important experiences with built architecture develop in their own first projects. Towards the end of an architectural career, the case base of an architect is large enough to be used efficiently.

The process of adaptation of existing architecture to new designs is a complex endeavor. A simple step is the null adaptation or the direct copy that – for legal and ethical considerations – rarely happens, unless it is a copy of one's own work. At the next level of abstraction, parts of architectural solutions are included in one's own design, others are adapted geometrically or according to material. In the most complex, but also most interesting form of adaptation, topological changes are applied. At the end of each adaptation, an evaluation follows to test whether the adaptation of the selected case leads to the required quality. The evaluation results in either the acceptance of the solution or in the return to an earlier phase of the selection or adaptation process.

Design Instrumentarium: Delegates and Agents

Delegates or agents contain knowledge, are designed to work on a specific task, can work autonomously, act on behalf of the user, and have the ability to learn. Agents are computer programs that attempt to solve problems that other programs cannot solve. Their purpose is to support the designer and the client. As an illustration of the work of agents and delegates is the typical cooperation between partners in the building process. Four types of agents support the individual actions.

The *presenter* agent autonomously presents data to the users in the appropriate format, for example, as text, tables, animations, or models. The *mediator* agent provides communication between the partners connected through the network. It provides access to audio, video and three-dimensional models and offers tools for cooperative work. It also supports agent-to-agent communication. The *representative* agent represents the user in the network towards other users, companies, and other agents. It autonomously reports on the activities of other participants. The *facilitator* looks for specified themes in the Internet. Acting as a crawler, it collects information, evaluates the reliability of the source and keeps the connection to the URL. It interprets vague information from the Internet and provides its findings to the presenter agent.

Functioning agents of this and similar types emerge in several research projects. One of them is the Information, Communication and Collaboration System (ICCS) for the building industry [http://caad.arch.ethz.ch/research/IuK]. Agents could guarantee that decision makers in the design and building process can concentrate on their core activities and rely on computer agents to take care of the more time consuming information-gathering and negotiation processes.

Design Instrumentarium: Sculptor

Sculptor is a program developed by David Kurmann at ETH Zürich to support the early conceptual phase of object and architectural design (Kurmann 1997, http://caad.arch.ethz.ch/~kurmann/sculptor). It allows intuitive interaction with a virtual model and is based on known concepts and mechanisms of spatial composition and recognition. *Sculptor* provides objects, models and worlds whose attributes and behavior – such as form, geometry, color, material, and movement – can be specified interactively, in addition to modeling constraints such as collision and gravity. Objects, groups of objects and worlds can be changed by scaling, translating, condensing, and exploding.

Besides the possibility of modeling with solid objects, *Sculptor* offers the opportunity to model with spatial elements, or voids. Such negative volumes that create a void when intersected with a solid can be manipulated and moved in the same manner as solids. Solids and voids have the same data structure. The interactive real-time intersection of positive and negative volumes supports the direct composition of spaces. This results in a freedom of modeling that has not been achieved so far with commercial programs. A third special type of objects in *Sculptor* are rooms, consisting of a solid and a contained space. The operations on rooms and spaces are fundamental in architecture and their availability in *Sculptor* greatly enhances the usefulness of the tool for architects. Rooms also have the advantage that a single additional attribute, the purpose of the room, puts necessary information into digital models, information that later can be interpreted by intelligent agents.

Sculptor's user interface allows the use of spatial-input devices. It encourages modeling and experiencing a building from the outside as well as from the inside, without the view being disturbed by too many buttons and dialog boxes. Spaces and objects can turn into dynamic design objects which act autonomously within specified constraints. The program thus becomes an interactive design aid, moving through different states, dynamically interpolating between possible design solutions. All solutions are syntactically correct, according to previously defined rules, but they have different qualities. The designer observes this autonomous movement and can stop it at any point. *Sculptor* has been integrated with the constraint and case-based architectural floor-planning software IDIOM (Smith 1996). An abstract graph of a floor plan can be generated, representing different rooms and their connections. The default, minimal, and maximal sizes of each space and the site can be specified either numerically or graphically in three dimensions. The result of the calculation of a dimensionality reduction algorithm (Faltings 1991) leads to a proposal for arranging spaces, which is read in *Sculptor* and displayed in three dimensions. The user can subsequently proceed with further refinement and experimentation with this model. *Sculptor* and IDIOM collaborate on one computer screen. All changes in the two-dimensional IDIOM interface are reflected directly in the three dimensional *Sculptor* interface and vice versa.

Distributed Sculptor is adding the possibility of Computer-

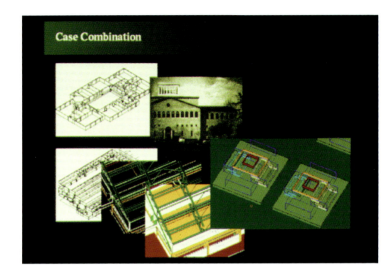

Case Combination

The stages of case combination. The architecture school in Houston, Texas (top), and the Graduate School of Design building at Harvard University (bottom) are automatically combined to propose the designs on the right. Bharat Dave, 1993.

supported Collaborative Design (CSCD) to *Sculptor* (Dave 1995). Different users on locally distributed computers share a 3D-model. Every user can have an individual point of view. The user holding the pen or modeling device is allowed to make changes, while the others may only observe. Each collaboration site enables observation of current sessions and allows users to join or create a new distributed cooperation session.

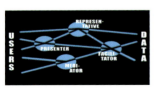

Four kinds of agents supporting the members of a virtual architectural firm: presenter, mediator, representative and facilitator.

Another possibility of CSCW is supported by translating *Sculptor* models into Virtual Reality Modeling Language (VRML) models, so that they can be accessed over the World Wide Web. There are plans to enhance the CSCW through a Collaboration Agent that helps to keep the model consistent and solves conflicts when different users want to access and modify the model simultaneously (Lashkari 1994).

Design Teaching: Informationslandschaft

First year architecture students need a continuously evolving CAAD education. It is not sufficient to teach basic CAD functionalities, or to teach a particular CAD package in-depth, as there are several dozen competing products on the market. Information technology use in architecture must be introduced to demonstrate the computer's possible role as a medium rather than just a tool. A particular approach to CAAD education is presented in *Architektur mit dem Computer* (Schmitt 1996a, http://caad.arch.ethz.ch/projects/acm), structured in chapters about information technology, building informatics, computer-aided architectural design, and architecture in the information territory. Based on experiences with this approach, Maia Engeli and her team developed a scheme for the first two years of architectural education, of which the first semester is named *Informationslandschaft* (information landscape), the second semester *Territorium* and the third semester has the title *Raumgeschichten* (stories of space).

More than 200 students work in *Informationslandschaft*. The 53 information landscape evolves on top of a clothing pattern, used at the same time as a starting point for the design education course and for the CAAD course. Students begin to draw and design on their individual site – named carpet – with a paint tool, exploring the borders between the individual carpets as lines of contact. The second exercise teaches how to establish electronic communication with the neighbors, used to negotiate common design strategies. The third exercise focuses on information search on the Internet. The last exercise involves the establishment of connections to external information and symbols.

Technically, a carpet contains information such as its position in the entire pattern and its modification date. Each carpet tuple also contains a field for the image map connecting the associated image with the WWW counterpart network the students are creating. This way, editing can take place inside the browser and changes to the image maps, such as the introduction of a mail link in the communication exercise, imply a simple update of all tuples by the course administrators [http://alterego.arch.ethz.ch/informationslandschaft].

Raumgeschichten

56 *Raumgeschichten,* or stories of space, is the title of a third-and-fourth-semester architecture CAAD course at ETH Zürich. The goal of the course was to communicate architectural ideas in a linear narrative manner, to be combined in the following semester into a large hyper document. Spatial stories were developed inside a frame: on the right side is a named link to go to the next frame, on the left side the one to move backwards. Text, images, animations or combinations of them occupy the center of the frame; some students also added sound. Each story has a name, stored as a hyperlink in the site. Its activation starts the story.

The relation to future architectural design practice is obvious: The story frames can serve as containers for design ideas. By navigating backwards and forwards through the data base, one can re-visit previous design decisions, add to them, or develop new branches. The multi-media character of the documents ensures that a complete textual, visual and audio record of design decisions is kept. The complete environment can be visited under [http://alterego.arch.ethz.ch/raumgeschichten].

Design Teaching: Phase(X)

57 Phase(X) is the first design course at ETH Zürich using the computer as a medium. It is the newest in a series of network-based teaching experiments which has involved more than 600 students since 1993. Its purpose is to pose and explore fundamental questions concerning design ideas, modeling and authorship. Phase(X) expands the idea of the paperless studio by building multi-dimensional computer models, by networking the designs and by focusing on abstract concepts, such as Types & Instances (Schmitt 1996a, p. 126). Adding modeling instruments such as Sculptor offered students additional opportunities to explore new design approaches, based on playful interaction with design objects.

Phase(X) treats authorship in a way that is only possible in a networked, cooperative design environment. After each phase, students do not proceed with their own design but continue with a solution that they carefully select from the results of their colleagues.

In Phase(1), they start with two-dimensional compositions on an empty grid and place the design into the Phase(X) data base. The result is immediately visible in a browser window. In Phase(2) and in all following phases, students can choose freely from the examples in the data base. They check out a design and continue to work on it. Students progressively refine the objects in the following design stages. The final results are complex objects with shared authorship that can be traced back to the contributing authors and co-authors. Two important views of the process and the products developed: InWorld and OutWorld.

InWorld describes the perspective of the participant from within the structure of the experiment. The interface places observer and designer in an introverted position. They can only see the direct vicinity of the design: its parent and its children. The system presents itself as a genetic tree structure, without horizon or perspective. Only navigation from branch to branch sheds some light on the system structure. The relations between objects, although rigidly maintained by the data base, remain subjectively connected only through the memories of individual images and models. InWorld is the plane on which design ideas are developed and stored. Phase(X) objectively keeps the memory of the individual designs and makes them available in real time. Out of this develops the OutWorld.

OutWorld is the name for the presentations that evolve from the entire data set. Based on these overviews, cross comparisons emerge, assumptions and theses can be explored. OutWorld replaces the sequential view of the InWorld with a parallel view. The interface produces the presentation – consisting of lines and surfaces in two- and three-dimensional space – in real time. The different overview presentations give partial objectivity to the OutWorld. The observer influences the views by choosing parameters.

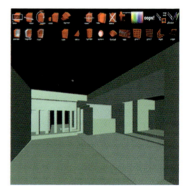

Left:Individual views of a collaborative Sculptor session appear in model and text windows. Right: The interface for designing with Sculptor from the inside out. David Kurmann, 1998.

Sculptor models rendered with Radiance in the Phase(X) course at ETH Zürich. Mark Frey (top) and Christoph Loppacher(bottom), 1996.

Image of Information-slandschaft six weeks after the beginning of the course. More than 200 individual designs have developed based on the original pattern. The web site is clickable and contains a wealth of Internet addresses related to architecture and art (http://alterego. arch.ethz.ch/informationslandschaft

More than 700 student works from one semester form a large quarry of design data.

Phase(X) introduces the notion of memes to design. We see memes as an analogy to genes (Dawkins 1976) that contain crucial information for the replication and development of organisms. We assume that designs contain memes that have different qualities: they may be strong, so a design is chosen by many others for further development in the next phase; they may be strong and sustainable, so they influence not only the next but also the following design stages. These qualities can be interactively explored in the Phase(X)2 interface (see *Design Teaching: Phase(X)2*).

Together, InWorld and OutWorld form an environment that could not be created or exist without the computer. They are therefore an example for the use of the computer as a medium. More important, working in the framework of *Phase(X)* leads students to better results in less time. The site can be visited and experienced under (http://space.arch.ethz.ch /ws96/).

Design Teaching: fake.space

60-61 *fake.space* is the name of a teaching system invented by Fabio Gramazio, Urs Hirschberg, Florian Wenz, Bige Tunçer and Cristina Besomi. Technically, it is a node system, consisting of different node types as containers for spatial descriptions and statements about space. All node types are represented as HTML documents, but they have different topics corresponding to the theme of the exercise in which they were introduced. Pipes and tanks were used as metaphors for the different functions any node in *fake.space* can assume. Tanks describe a spatial situation using a combination of floor plans, perspectives, light simulations, text, images and sound. Pipes have the function of demonstrating the content connection and the path between spaces. This important role as a mediator between different spaces is achieved with text. Starting from a central ring of nodes (the *fake.space* connector), new nodes can be added to any existing node, based on their content. *fake.space* is therefore constantly growing. The InWorld view is that of moving through tanks and pipes. The OutWorld view is that of exploring the data base.

In a first exercise, students connect an interior space, represented as a model, and an exterior space, represented as a path description. They achieve this by modeling their own apartment in plan view and in three dimensions. They add visual content with Photoshop. Then they look for a place in the system where they want to add their tank containing the model with a (text) pipe. A second exercise deals with insights and views to the outside, represented with 3D models and photographs. Students can freely choose the number of nodes they need to present their design. They can develop linear strings of information or include forks. They can react to an existing node by continuing the same theme, by adding detail, or by taking a contrasting standpoint.

The designs inside the tanks are represented as effectively lit Inventor models, complemented by scanned images and video clips. A third exercise focuses on the realistic simulation of light and atmosphere in the models to support the design story, using Radiance in combination with DIPAD, a program originally developed to aid in the semi-automatic photogrammetric measurement of buildings (Hirschberg and Streilein, 1996). The fourth exercise explores the type and quality of the circulation space which is of fundamental importance in *fake.space*, as each pipe or tank is part of the circulation space. To support this exercise, we developed a turtle array function that parametrically repeats circulation elements.The fifth exercise is dedicated to animation, using DIPAD and *Sculptor* to define and calculate the animation path through the design space. In the sixth exercise, an interior space is designed with *Sculptor* as reflection of the animation path. For the last exercise, we built a visitor's guide tool to define continuous paths through *fake.space*. The tool also allows visitors to be brought directly to interesting places and to suggest paths through the data base. This creates a meta-level navigation system on top of the existing data base.

Common to all exercises is that students work in asynchronous mode, and then upload the result, which can immediately be experienced by all other participants. The OutWorld data base representation itself took on an aesthetic quality which inspired the navigation through tanks and nodes. Once

RAUMGESCHICHTEN

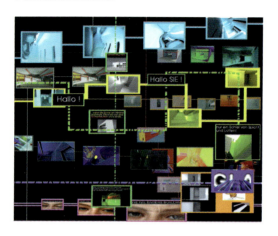

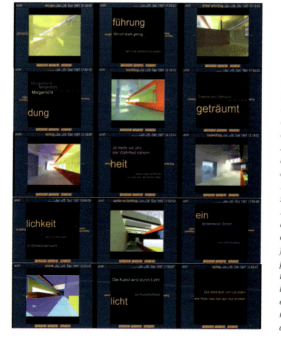

Top: The image of Raumgeschichten demonstrates the linear character and the connections of the spatial stories (http:// alterego.arch.ethz.ch /raumgeschichten). Left: "Jenseits," one spatial story from Raumgeschichten in detail. The frames contain a text link from the previous part of the story on the left and the text link to the next part of the story on the right (http:// alterego. arch.ethz.ch).

PHASE(X)

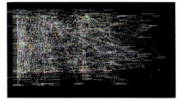 

Top: Four views of the same database. Projects ordered by genealogy and author (top left), authors and connections (top right), authors and connections and time (below left), and genealogy, author and quality (below right).

Bottom: Phase(X) designer and user interface. Top level menu frame on the left. Main window with ancestor project (left), focus of interest (center) and follow-up projects (right). Scrollable project database frame at the bottom. F. Wenz, F. Gramazio, U. Hirschberg, P. Sibenaler, C. Besomi, B. Tunçer, 1996.

on the InWorld level, the spatial quality and the lighting and material simulation further encourage navigation and experience of *fake.space*. The complete site can be visited under [http:// space.arch.ethz.ch/ss97/].

Design Teaching: Phase(X)2

64 *Phase(X)2* is the sequel to *Phase(X)*, with many improvements in the interface and the data base. Whereas *Phase(X)* used a modified AutoCAD as modeling program, *Phase(X)2* is based on MicroStation. The procedure of designing is similar: Phase(1) - Composition in the plane, Phase(2) - Objects in the plane, Phase(3) - Positive and negative volumes, Phase(4) - Rotation in space and movement, Phase(5) - Freeform surfaces – structure and cover, Phase(6) - Design vocabulary, Phase(7) - Parametric solids, Phase(8) - Self-similar structures and fractals, Phase(9) - Light and space.

A major difference to *Phase(X)* is that the OutWorld – the data base overview – can be seen immediately and concurrently with the InWorld – the individual projects. In addition, new views on the data base are enabled. Users can choose to see the most recent entries in each phase; they can look at the most relevant designs in terms of memes and followers; they can rate designs according to their criteria and see the overall ratings of each project; they can study the time it took to generate a specific design; they can explore the data base according to certain key words. They can also have a quick overview of the work of an individual designer. The complete data base can be visited under [http://space.arch .ethz.ch/ws97/].

Judging from the students' and the teachers' response, this new way of teaching and learning design is attractive. The fact that no individual ownership of a design is possible seems not to pose a problem to anyone. Perhaps this is due to the fact that the university environment is not as competitive as professional practice, and that the designs were of an abstract nature. All the people asked could imagine working in practice under similar conditions. Therefore, Phase(X) might be a strong hint to the future architectural working environment. To test this hypothesis, we conducted the *Multiplying time* experiment to introduce a real design problem, along with some working conditions closer to architectural practice (see *Multiplying time*).

Virtual architecture: the computer as partner and its impact on future architecture

Designing in the information territory leads to virtual architecture and as such to a radical alternative to existing, physical architecture. In this territory, information is the raw material and the only reality is a virtual one. The computer is at the same time instrument, infrastructure and design environment. It has received the role as a partner that is able to accept responsibilities and to execute certain tasks independently.

Design in the information territory will rely on similar methods and instruments as conventional computer-aided architectural design. Methods are in particular abstraction, generation of models, and simulation (Schmitt 1996a, p. 154). But, contrary to using a computer in a conventional design process, the creation of physical structures is not the main purpose. Rather, the goal is to overcome typical shortcomings of physical architecture. For example, virtual structures consume much less energy than building and maintaining physical structures, and virtual conferences result in less transportation and energy consumption than conventional meetings (see *Quality of life in the information territory*). At the same time, the advantages of personal meetings and of physical architectural environments must not be lost.

Design with the computer as partner in the information territory is a mental activity for which computing offers fundamental methods and instruments. In this modeling territory of thought – a human invention – the designer meets computer-based modeling instruments that are also human inventions. In this abstract world of ideas, man and machine can achieve a high degree of compatibility. It can lead to significant improvements of the design process and ultimately to better physical design, if there is sufficient feedback from virtual structures and virtual architecture developed for and in the information

60

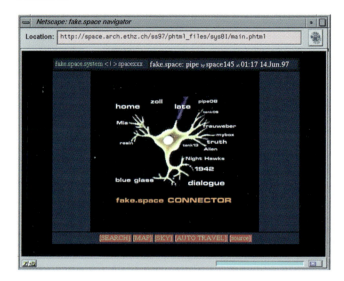

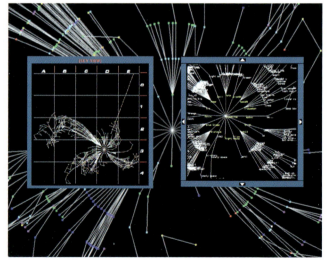

Top: The connector as the structural and organizational idea behind fake.space (http://space.arch.ethz.ch/ss97). Bottom: fake.space OutWorld view with three differently scaled views of the data base.

Top: fake.space interface with an array of spatial descriptions. Each frame represents a participant in the fake.space studio.

Bottom: Memes and quality. Note that the projects rated best in quality do not necessarily have the most follow-ups.

territory. Working in the information territory must not result in a humanization of the machine or a computerization of humans. The information territory is a neutral, abstract region to which both man and machine have access. In this environment, the computer becomes a natural, intellectual partner.

Information as raw material

The importance of raw materials such as water, wood, oil or iron is decreasing in post-industrial countries, whereas the role of information as a raw material is increasing. Seen by itself, information is as useless as a piece of ore, but processed and placed in the appropriate context where it can be used, it has far-reaching effects.

Information consists of structured data recorded on storing devices. To transport and exchange information, an infrastructure is necessary. In the early days of electronic data exchange, one relied on the conventional physical infrastructure, such as streets and trains. Data were copied on a disk or tape, then packaged and sent by mail. In practice, it makes less and less sense to move data to an external medium first, to mail this medium, and later bring the content back on a second computer, because networks have developed in which data can freely flow between all nodes.

In the 18th and 19th century, industrialists became rich by refining raw material. Tremendous fortunes were made in railway and street construction, when the task was to develop infrastructure for the transport and refinement of raw materials. A parallel development could be observed with computer firms. The situation repeats itself today with organizations that offer information infrastructure.

In most industrialized countries, information transport was a very profitable state monopoly until the opening of the telecommunication markets. With the disappearance of these monopolies, competition is increasing, resulting for clients in lower costs, but also in some confusion about the multitude of new services.

Common to all these developments is the increasing importance of knowing how to find and retrieve information, rather than to have information stored in memory or on a local machine. The non-physical place where the new raw material can be mined and processed is the Internet. This place is perceived wherever a connection is available.

The information territory

The expression information territory is somehow a contradiction of terms, as in the emerging information age, most of the territories known today – such as private territories, military territories, or national territories – lose their original meaning. But it is useful as a description of a future design territory that has in some respects similar properties as existing territories. The information territory is populated by people with access to a node of a computer network. Forms of access control, of privileges, and of new rules are under development for the information territory. With the proliferation of data connections through cable or satellite even in remote areas of the world, access becomes easier. But access and bandwidth are available only to those with the privilege of being able to afford them financially. The reach of the Internet defines the limits of the information territory. Rules are emerging rapidly, and a different net etiquette develops every few months. Increasingly, commercial and political sources attempt to take control of the new territory.

Internet and World Wide Web

The Internet has been one of the most frequently used terms in research, education and the media since the middle of the 1990s. It is accessible to anyone with a computer and at least a modem. The number of persons connected to the Internet is growing rapidly and will exceed 100 million by the end of the century. The Internet connects people from all cultures, all nations, across the world. It has existed for a long time in other, more primitive forms. It underwent the same development as the telephone networks. It started with two machines sending data to each other, but evolved quickly into a worldwide network. In a telephone network it is possible to call anyone anytime with a single number. In the Internet it is possible to reach everyone with a unique address. But in addition, the Internet is a giant data base. Given enough bandwidth, it

PHASE(X)2

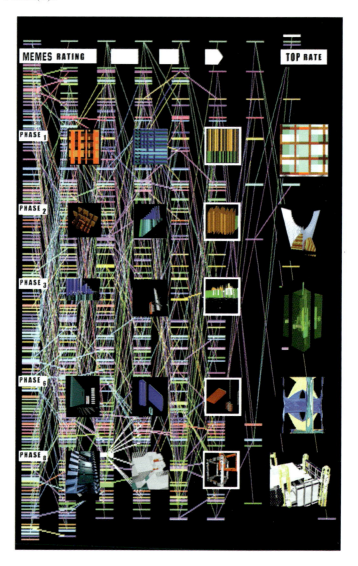

VIRTUAL ARCHITECTURE

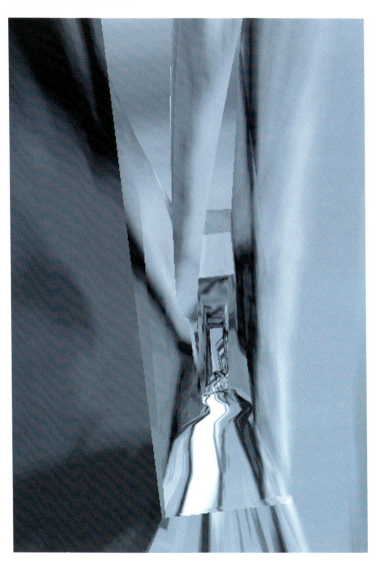

Virtual Architecture: the computer as partner and its impact on future architecture.
Center for Cognitive Imagination, Malgorzata Miskiewicz-Bugajski.

also allows person-to-person communication through voice, video or exchange of models.

The development of the World Wide Web (WWW) started in 1989, when Tim Berners-Lee and his colleagues at CERN, the European research center near Geneva, defined a protocol for the standardization of communication between servers and clients. They called it Hyper Text Transfer Protocol (HTTP). The World Wide Web became attractive very quickly with the appearance of the web browser *Mosaic*, which was developed in the United States by Marc Andreesen and others at the National Center for Supercomputer Applications of the University of Illinois. The first publication followed in September 1993. *Mosaic* used the point and click paradigm which simplified access to information dramatically and made it available to a large number of users. In April of 1994, Marc Andreesen was co-founder of Netscape Communication Corporation.

The Netscape Navigator was released in 1994 and quickly captured the majority of users worldwide. A year later, Microsoft Corporation started to develop its own browser, the Internet Explorer. The so-called browser wars since the middle of the 1990s demonstrate the importance of this new territory for electronic commerce.

Space in the Internet

The Internet as a worldwide information base and communication system redefines the notion of space in at least two ways. Hyperlinked documents and data bases allow us to take virtual journeys to any place in the world at any time, if data about it exists on the Internet. In addition, new browsers allow three- and more-dimensional representations of artifacts.

Space in the Internet can be described with – among other things – text, images, multi-dimensional models and sound. Documents are described in the Hyper Text Markup Language (HTML) that allows the easy and platform-independent exchange of information in a standardized format. Text descriptions can be hyper-linked into intricate constructs that describe space purely with words, as numerous virtual meeting spaces on the Internet demonstrate.

They are known as Multi-User Domains, or MUDs, and are developing into a field of architectural research.

In addition to text and images, browsers can display three-dimensional models. Models are described with the Virtual Reality Modeling Language (VRML), an evolving standard that could transform the way we experience three- and more-dimensional space. With VRML models, different kinds of information can be combined to visualize interdependencies. It is possible, for example, to combine a Geographic Information System (GIS) data base with building models from other parts of the world and to display both models together in VRML on the Internet.

This development has added a new meaning to the notion of space. The architectural space as we know it from physical environments is supplemented by a virtual space. Physical, architectural and virtual space share very similar results in simulation: once on a computer display or in a virtual environment, the simulation of a real space becomes indistinguishable from the simulation of an abstract space on the Internet.

In VRML models, the boundary between the representation

In Dataspace, interactive data structures are represented by three-dimensional geometric descriptions and information mapping. A random-access structure and a data array are connected by a sequential strip and the interior bounding surfaces of the data array are entirely covered by mapped information. Florian Wenz, 1993.

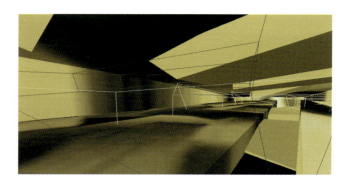

Center for Cognitive Imagination – information space which can be perceived interactively through different motion patterns assigned to the VRML model [http://caad.arch.ethz.ch/teaching/nds/program/thesis/projects.html]. Malgorzata Miskiewicz-Bugajski, 1997.

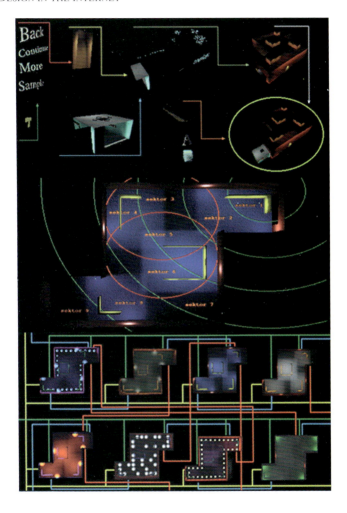

Aquamicans, a virtual high-rise building with 51 rooms constructed in VRML, is organized around a surrealistic text by Raymond Roussel (Roussel 1989, chapter 3). The rooms, which always have the same geometry, receive their interior charac-ter through lighting variations and are linked by 4 doors each and one elevator. The possible floor plans of the entire construct are created during interactive explo-ration and only exist in the user's imagination. Fabio Gramazio (etoy), 1995.

of physical sites and imaginary, virtual sites is vanishing rapidly, resulting in a new reality (Fünfschilling 1992).

Communication in the Internet

Communication was a main purpose of the Internet from the very beginning. Starting with researchers who wanted to transmit and discuss results, the potential for communication through computer networks was recognized quickly by the general public when the first useful browsers emerged. Since then, communication using text, models, sound, and video has become a key point of interest in using the Internet. As could be expected, the Internet is beginning to fundamentally change communication itself. Written and spoken communication have not lost their proven value, but they are now supported and supplemented by the crucial capability of the Internet to access information and people worldwide and to communicate on several new channels.

The only type of communication that does not require technical infrastructure is face-to-face communication. But even this type of communication requires the knowledge of a common language. All other forms of communication are based on technical media for transmission and reception.

The main difference between the Internet and conventional media, such as television, radio or newspapers, is that it is just no longer a few organizations that provide information. Instead, all people with access to the Internet are potential content providers. This may lead to a situation where there are as many listeners as there are producers of information. Therefore, the Internet is the first technical medium that actually enables communication rather than transmitting filtered observations and opinions from few information providers to millions of listeners or viewers. It will take a few years until this difference is generally recognized and appreciated. But it is the main advantage of the Internet over all other existing means of technical communication.

Internet-based communication will change the character of space and architecture in many ways: the individual work place will have to accommodate communication equipment; electronic communication rooms will emerge as a new type of space; and even urban planning will have to react to the changing nature of communication.

Design in the Internet

Architectural design is the art of producing a solution based on incomplete descriptions of a problem or a desire. The proposal may result in physical artifacts, or in other useful objects and functions. Design has always relied on instruments and external media – such as paper – to transmit the designer's ideas to the client, and in particular to the crafts persons necessary to execute the design (McCullough 1996). The influence of instruments on the designed artifact itself is undisputed. The Internet has become the design site for all those who are interested in building in the information territory. The needs of the information society will demonstrate that design no longer results in physical artifacts alone. Instead, the new design will produce structures that can be simulated perfectly with computer media and which only exist in a computer network. A viewer will not be able to differentiate between the representation of physical architecture and the representation of a proposed design in a computer, unless she or he knows the actual building or city which is represented in the first place. Thus, the relation between representation and architecture will be much closer in the information territory than in the physical world.

Construction in the Internet

Few of the many publications about the Internet describe the very interesting possibility of building virtual structures. If we assume that future reality is increasingly influenced by the reality of the Internet and other virtual media, then construction on the Internet will be a real business in the near future. Writers and researchers have pointed to developments in this direction over the last years. The traditional building and facade of a bank in main street is increasingly replaced by automated teller machines (ATMs) that can be placed anywhere where money is needed (Mitchell 1995). The architectural result is the proliferation of relatively inexpensive machines in many parts of a city and in the countryside,

CONSTRUCTION IN THE INTERNET

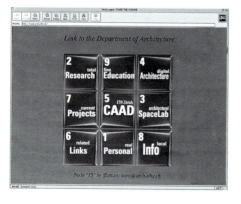

Three generations of web designs on the same construction site in the Internet [http://caad.arch.ethz.ch/]. The first design (bottom) by Florian Wenz dates from 1993. This web site is already historic and had to be reconstructed from backup tapes of these years by Malgorzata Bugajski. The second design (center) dates from 1995-1998 by Eric van der Mark. The third design is the first three-dimensional web site from 1998, by Maria Papanikolaou.

The etoy tank system as a construction metaphor in the Internet. For the group etoy (digital highjack 1996, Golden Nica, Ars Electronica 1996), the tank system fulfills the functions of a conventional office, information and entertainment center, and more. etoy, 1995.

whereas the large physically present and personnel-intensive banks are slowly disappearing. The next logical step is that the entrance to a bank will not be the physical facade or even the ATM anymore, but its two- or three-dimensional information structure on the Internet. It is foreseeable that the corporate identity of a bank and other businesses will be increasingly influenced by their appearance on the Internet.

Construction on the Internet has already begun in several areas. The variety in displaying ideas and products – even if constrained to two-dimensional pages and images – is fascinating. Fashion designers have invented different aesthetics than universities. Car manufacturers advertise their product in another way than service providers. Newspapers reconstruct their front pages to facilitate access through the Internet. It might in fact be more interesting for a fashion company to build interactive, three-dimensional structures on the Internet, rather than renting expensive physical storefronts. Furniture companies and computer stores feature outlets with three-dimensional models of the artifacts that the clients can configure and order on-line. For universities, the Internet can replace parts of the library, for car dealers the show room, for newspapers the newsstand.

These cases demonstrate that the new technology, used appropriately, will impact design and construction. In the past, physical materials determined architecture and urban space; later, it was the constraints of style and gravity. These constraints have disappeared in the information territory and are replaced by the human capacity to perceive.

Design and construction in the information territory are by no means easier than on physical properties. In both cases, construction must be carefully prepared. There is nothing more disappointing than a badly designed web site, and it does as much damage to the owner of the web site as a badly designed and maintained building does to the owner of the store. Construction costs in the Internet are still much lower than in physical reality, but the clients' requirements for perfect sites are rising rapidly. This will in turn increase the cost of Internet design. As in the physical world, designers and contractors have opened their businesses in the information territory. Similar to the physical world, many sites are cluttered with advertisement billboards that appear in between news and other information. In the long run, it will be as difficult to keep the Internet free of commercial overcrowding as it is in the real world. One will probably have to pay more for advertisement-free zones in the future.

The future architecture in the information territory

Simulation of future architecture in the information territory offers the possibility of avoiding some of those characteristics of physical architecture that have been recognized as detrimental to the environment or to the comfort of the inhabitants. We are so accustomed to the constraints of conventional territories that the disappearance of those constraints causes some real problems. For example, what does it mean when information needs no physical means to be transported? What does it mean when people do not need to move physically to their offices during most of the week anymore? What does it mean when gravity is no issue? The answers to these questions will shape the future architecture and the future city.

Several designers and researchers have addressed these questions. John Frazer, Head of the School of Design at the Hong Kong Polytechnic University, has investigated alternative forms of cities and buildings for a number of years and summarized his thoughts in the book *An Evolutionary Architecture* (Frazer 1995). William Mitchell has written extensively about the future city in the information territory in *City of Bits* (Mitchell 1995). Christine Boyer goes beyond the description of future cybercities and issues a call to reinstall a social agenda to avoid "becoming incapable of action in a real city plagued by crime, hatred, disease, unemployment and undereducation" (Boyer 1996).

In practice, large numbers of people do already populate the information territory in simulated architecture and cities. The Telepolis project in Luxembourg in November 1995 opened new insights into the feasibility and problems of virtual cities [http://www./rz-muenchen.de/~MLM/telepolis/english/telepolis.html]. There are Internet sites that provide virtual three-dimensional landscapes and meeting places, even used for design competitions [http://www.ccon.org/theU /index.html]. And finally, thousands of copies of Sim City, Myst, or Riven have brought the idea of a virtual city and landscape to the general public.

All theories on future architecture and on ideal cities in the past used conventional graphics and written text to depict and to create in the viewers' mind the best possible image of the new city. To describe the future architecture in the information territory, computer graphics is the medium of choice. In addition to the pictorial quality of conventional media, computer graphics and digital models allow a significant depth of information associated with the graphical or written element. They also allow interactive communication with the model.

The design and construction of future architecture and cities is not restricted to a few city planners and architects anymore, but taken seriously; a large portion of the population can take part in this exercise through the Internet. An example is the interactive presentation accompanying the exhibition *The Archaeology of the Future City* at the Museum of

Contemporary Art in Tokyo, which was accessible on the Internet [http://caad.arch.ethz.ch/trace].

Sustainable development in the information territory

Structures in the information territory are by orders of magnitude more sustainable than conventional, physically-based environments, if the definition of sustainability in the Brundtland Report is applied (World Commission 1987):

> A process of change in which the exploitation of resources, the direction of investments, the orientation of technological development, and institutional change are all in harmony and enhance both the current and future potential to meet human needs and aspirations.

The construction of virtual architecture and cities in the information territory must not destroy the cultural achievements of physical architecture and cities of the past. To meet the social and ethical requirements of sustainability, it will not be enough to create virtual spaces and structures, but they must connect with physical, real places.

The importance of design quality in the physical environment will increase with the settlement of the information territory. This process can be compared with the discovery and development of the Americas from the 15th to the 19th century. The new settlers brought crucial ideas and techniques from Europe, but that did not inhibit the emergence of a new and local culture, separated from their countries of origin. And also, the Old World did not disintegrate or deteriorate after the discovery of the New World. In analogy, every new settler and building in the information territory increases the chances for a sustainable development in the traditional territories.

Quality of life in the information territory

Quality of life means access to and distribution of the essential physical and intellectual resources needed to survive and to enjoy life. Living and working in the information territory primarily means a shift from physical possessions towards information transactions and knowledge. Predictions extend to the replacement of money with attention as the currency of the future.

The reduction of physical travel is one example how the quality of life could improve in the information territory. Working at home could mean a reduction in traffic pollution and other negative side effects of mobility. But estimates predict only a 3-5% drop in traffic pollution, because often more communication is accompanied by more travel as well [http://www.lrz-muenchen.de/~MLM/telepolis/deutsch/thinktank/ levycy. htm]. In addition, recent studies have shown that women and men who work exclusively at home with telecommunication to their offices will not be able to socialize and move up in the career hierarchy as quickly.

A common critique of the new development is that personal relations could suffer with the emergence of the information age. This in turn would be a loss in the quality of life. Yet most of this critique ignores the fact that the new information technology offers the possibility of a truly new way to communicate. It will be not a replacement of conventional communication, but a welcome expansion to conventional

An InWorld view in TRACE. Textures mapped on the walls of a corridor connecting nodes are selected based on the previous behavior of the visitor. The corridor exists only during the time of navigation. Florian Wenz and Fabio Gramazio, 1996.

forms of communication for several groups of a society, including children, managers, elderly people or the handicapped. Each group can and will use the new technology in their own way. Breaking down traditional barriers between groups could indeed improve the quality of life for their members and for society in general.

Electronic media increasingly render the conventional transmission of documents, letters and other information obsolete. In many cases, fax and electronic mail have replaced the telegram and the written letter. But none of the previous means of communication have disappeared entirely.

Therefore, we can expect that many aspects of working and living in the information territory will be similar to the present situation, but that many of the time-consuming, physically straining or dangerous activities, such as driving or flying, can be reduced.

To understand the consequences of the new medium, it is useful to observe people who already live and work in this environment – people who spend more than a few hours per day in the information territory. Those people, mostly located in universities and other high-tech environments, are still a minority and might therefore not correctly predict the future development of society in general.

It seems indeed a danger that the information territory could become so attractive that people of a certain age group and profession get totally drawn into it and start to neglect and ignore their physical environment, along with the people who populate it. Hopefully this will be the exception and not the norm.

A global economy has developed and is in operation already. Today, the energy sector and the telecommunication business are two of the worldwide dominating economic forces. An increase in telecommunication might reduce the energy needed to produce the artifacts of the future. Vice versa, the reduction of energy costs might reduce the need for developing better telecommunication devices. Once some of the office and other light industrial work can be replaced by electronic means and by simulation, the need for large office spaces and production facilities will decrease. This will require an architectural re-thinking of the quality of the places where people work and live during the day.

TRACE City

The design and construction of a new city in the information territory is an occasion where humans and machine must interact as partners. The opportunity for this experiment came with the exhibition *The Archaeology of the Future City* that opened in July 1996 in the Museum of Contemporary Art in Tokyo (MOCA 1996). Florian Wenz and Fabio Gramazio developed *TRACE*, an interactive computer installation. There was purposely no attempt to reconstruct visionary city models of the past. *TRACE* was built to pre- **81** sent and test ideas concerning the virtual aspects of cities. The location of the city is the Internet, the material is information, the builders and inhabitants are the visitors of the exhibition.

The interaction between known systems – such as a city – and virtual systems – such as the Internet – is not well understood; as they do not share a common language which could describe phenomena in both systems. Virtual reality environments must mediate between those two worlds. *TRACE* generates spaces by registering activities of local and networked visitors, by interpreting and representing them (Wenz and Gramazio 1996). The activities of the virtual city's visitors generate structural substance – the code of the space. Therefore, *TRACE* originates from the energy or motivation of the visitors to present themselves in the environment, to leave traces and to read and interpret traces of previous visitors.

The space develops further by a constant information exchange between a data base and a geometry generator. The data base saves the traces with the help of an event agent, a program that acts on behalf of the visitor. The geometry generator translates the traces into perceivable, three-dimensional spaces. The visitor experiences space in two different time axes: in synchronous real time as the condition of the system at the time of logging on, and as an evolving system time in the asynchronous superposition of the visitor's activities.

TRACE uses an abstracting architectural syntax in the form

QUALITY OF LIFE IN THE INFORMATION TERRITORY

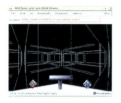 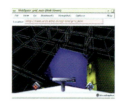 

Matrix 3.O creates spatial user representations by combining vertical and horizontal elements, logos and quotes into unique, personalized spatial fabrics. This architectural syntax machine is accessible over the Internet and uses VRML.

 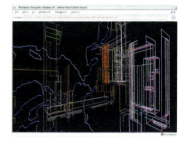

Hollow Planet is a virtual urban construction site, created by remote participants over the Internet. The sectors of Hollow Planet are in the center of an outlined Planet Earth, whose continents are visible from anywhere. They replace the horizontal reference plane of the horizon and express the concept of a completely self-contained system, which can evolve independently of the constraints of the physical world. Online information at [http://caad.arch.ethz.ch/~wenz/babylon]. Florian Wenz, 1996.

Center for Cognitive Imagination – a space where the structure will allow information access by using different movement patterns. Interactive NDS CAAD thesis project at ETH Zürich. Malgorzata Miskieiwcz-Bugajski, 1997.

TRACE CITY

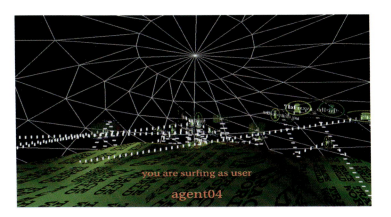

Top: A view of the TRACE interface. The private_in.world is the navigation space of connecting and containing nodes. Florian Wenz and Fabio Gramazio, 1996. Bottom: The public_out.world of TRACE, an overview that shows the growing city of information. Florian Wenz and Fabio Gramazio, 1996.

of icons to demonstrate specific aspects of the entire system. The spatial icons represent the actions of the visitors and the resulting matrix of impressions. The two fundamental forms of interaction in *TRACE* are abstract in exterior, public spaces and immersive in interior, private spaces.

Following the metaphor of the city, *TRACE* replaces the urban fabric of a private and public space by a dialectic system of two complementary spatial experiences, public_out.world and private_in.world. These are at the same time separated and networked. Both represent interaction, navigation, geometry and aesthetics in different ways. *TRACE* is not a simulation, although it uses methods and instruments of simulation. It is, in the sense of Jean Baudrillard, a substitution of the real (Baudrillard 1985).

The visitor and builder enters *TRACE* through one of many possible variations of public_out.world. The navigation space consists of a deformable, closed volume (blob), generated by a single folded surface that in its ideal state has the shape of a sphere. The actual form of the blob is defined by a fluid balance between pulling and pushing forces, which press as symbolized Internet sites after the user logs off on the control points of the surface. The visitor intuitively perceives the shape of the underlying surface during navigation while never actually seeing it. The system is scalable and it has no noticeable external limitations, such as a beginning or an end. In this public_out.world the visitors leave traces.

In contrast to public_out.world as complex superpositions, private_in.world is specific and seemingly simple. Here, the geometry generator translates traces of previous visitors in a network of containers with connecting corridors. Containers hold one unit of media (image, sound, model or text), while the connections contain a specific pattern of movement (straight, zigzag, up and down, curved). The user is caught in this labyrinth and navigates through it by moving continuously forward and by choosing in each container one of four options: straight ahead, back, right or left. A move backwards stops the generation cycle and releases the visitor back to the public_out.world, which now contains its previously created traces. A more complete description of the

TRACE environment can be found under [http://caad.arch. ethz.ch/trace]. Many of the ideas developed and tested in *TRACE* can be found in and stem from the work of the group etoy [http://www.etoy.com/].

Architecture and urbanism revisited

Cities and buildings were made of physical materials in the past. Instruments were made of physical material as well. In the information age, both instruments and buildings will have a higher information content, as information is the new material. Information is also an additional dimension of architecture. This duality in the meaning of information will have a fundamental impact on future design and on the built environment – architecture and the city.

The new role of information as medium and as raw material – with the computer and the network as the information processing infrastructure –– will make many of our previous concepts of architecture obsolete. It will change meanings more than it already has in the early years of computerization: a bank is no longer a bank, a university no longer a university, a store no longer a store. Unnoticed by most, a new infrastructure has developed through which most of the business transactions occur. It is invisible and superimposed on the physical infrastructure. Out of this, three scenarios develop: (i) the physical infrastructure will degrade and only point-to-point connections will survive, (ii) the physical and the information infrastructure will co-exist without influencing each other, or (iii) the information infrastructure will mature to a degree that it will improve the physical infrastructure.

In the first scenario, financial means will concentrate in fewer and fewer centers, and the areas around these centers will increasingly degrade as they are cut off from the main raw material: information. In the second scenario, the coexistence that we observe already today in the post-industrial countries will continue. We favor, of course, the last option. Parallels in history exist: southern England, originally intensively farmed, became the almost park-like landscape we know and appreciate today only after enough wealth was generated through the, then new, international trade infrastructure.

84

A new citizenship evolves with its own means of transportation, communication and commerce, named "netizen" by WIRED magazine as a prominent promoter of this idea. Those *connected* and *super connected* could be just another target group in the ever-increasing marketing efforts, or it could be a truly new nation of ideas coming into existence. Those people would be least likely to live in virtual buildings but, judging from the past, would do everything to live in luxurious but conventional architecture. This, in turn, would give the physical architecture an even higher degree of importance than before: in the sea of change, it would be the only remaining constant which memories and people refer to. Yet physical and virtual architecture have entered a state of symbiosis. Information has irreversibly expanded the dimensionality of architecture.

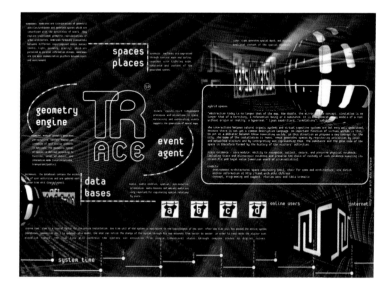

Conceptual and functional schema of TRACE, an autonomous urban process field.
Florian Wenz and Fabio Gramazio, 1996.

Glossary

Agent
Denotes a possibly intelligent tool or program as an aid or competent partner helping to perform various tasks on and with computers. For example, it buys the cheapest opera ticket online or reserves a hotel room. As of today, the agent community has not yet come up with a really intelligent, helpful agent used in everyday life.

Applets
Special, very small applications downloaded over the Internet that execute locally on a computer, typically inside a Web browser. Applets may be written in Java. Security measures make sure that any such applet is prevented from destroying the local system or data contained thereon.

Browser
A tool used to view pages and audio/video content published on the WWW. Browsers often include support for e-mail and electronic newsgroups. Common browsers in 1998 are Netscape Communicator and Microsoft Internet Explorer.

C++
Object-oriented programming language. Programs written in C++ are usually very fast but not portable, as Java programs are. On the WWW, C++ programs are mainly used by Web servers to compute dynamic WWW pages.

Data base
Special programs used to store data and access it quickly using specialized languages (the most common is SQL). Data bases are the key for the management of large data sets and are used in almost every company and recently by Web servers to make information available on the WWW.

Definitions
More definitions of terms can be found under the following addresses: Hotwired/Web101 magazine: http://www.hotwired.com/web101/. Microsoft: http://home.microsoft.com/exploring/exploring.asp. Yahoo search engine (man-made overview): http://www.yahoo.com/

E-mail or electronic mail
A service offered by the Internet, used to send electronic messages. In general, digital information (audio, video, and others) to a person or a group of people, who can then send a reply.

Electronic newsgroups or newsgroups or usenet
Service of the Internet. Discussion groups where people discuss a topic of their interest. There are discussion groups for almost every topic you can imagine. Also often dubbed USENET (actually just a subset, albeit the largest, of all newsgroups available).

Home page
A web page of a private person or netizen on the WWW. To publish a home page, a machine connected to the Internet or a provider is needed.

HTML
The language of the WWW. Pages published on the World Wide Web have to be written in HTML in order to be displayable by Web browsers. HTML is easy to learn and can be used to write private home pages.

HTTP
Strictly speaking, not a language, but a protocol. HTTP is used to transmit WWW pages written in HTML over the Internet. One does not need to know much about it when the intent is to simply publish pages on the WWW.

Internet
A global information network connecting approx. 20 million machines and 100 million users in 1998. The common denominator for all machinery connected to the Internet is the low-level protocol ("language") TCP/IP. The Internet uses phone lines, satellite links, special high-capacity wires and other connections to link its machines.

Java
New language used to write programs and applets. The unique feature of Java is its portability: once written, a Java program can run on any machine with Java support (for example, in the form of a Web browser with built-in Java).

Modem
Special device connected to a computer that transfers digital data over standard phone lines originally deployed for voice services only. A modem is needed to connect to a provider which in turn is connected to the Internet.

MSQL and MySQL
Two popular, small, fast data bases used on the WWW (see also: data bases). Both are free for non-commercial users.

Netizen

Short for network citizen. Someone who uses the WWW very frequently and allows it to change his or her way of life. Some people believe that the netizen is the future citizen. A future citizen, aware of the cultural and political diversity offered by the many cultures on this planet and willing to change the way things work.

Network computer

Special type of computer that is connected to a network (for example, the Internet) at all times. The idea is to free users from installing and updating software. Instead, network computers download tools and programs whenever needed and remove them after usage.

Perl

Programming language popular among WWW page designers, who need to write dynamic WWW pages. Perl is also useful for other purposes than publishing on the WWW.

PHP/FI

Like Perl, a programming language used by WWW page designers. PHP/FI is embedded (put) into HTML pages, the Web server runs these PHP/FI programs before sending the WWW page to the client, thus enabling a designer to write dynamic WWW pages.

Plug-in or helper applications

As the information on the WWW comes in many different types (audio, video, animation, 3D worlds) and these in turn in many different formats, plug-ins or helper applications are needed to interpret and visualize this information. Plug-ins and helper applications can be added to an already existing Web browser.

Provider

Organization or company offering access to the Internet to those who cannot afford linking their machine to the Internet 24 hours a day. Service providers have to be paid. Their machines, where for example private WWW pages reside, can be reached through normal phone lines. A computer and a modem are needed to connect to a provider.

Search engines or search services

As there is no central directory on the Internet containing a list of all public WWW pages, search engines or software robots are needed to constantly search the net and add links to an index. Common search engines in 1998 are: Hotbot, Altavista, Lycos, Yahoo, and InfoSeek.

Server/Client

In machine-to-machine communication, the machine serving information is the "server" and the machine receiving it the "client." Usually, servers are large protected systems and clients are on the users' desk. As an example, on the WWW, Web servers send the WWW documents to your machine, the client, where a tool, the browser, displays them.

Static and dynamic WWW pages

Pages written in HTML are called static. These only change if the HTML code is changed. Languages that are first composed by the Web server using specialized languages as Perl or PHP/FI are called dynamic. They do not exist as pages as such, but are computed each time they are accessed. Dynamic pages are essential to provide information stored in a database.

Virtual firm

A set of individual firms who get together to actively pursue a common goal, for example, a building project. The firms are electronically linked.

Virtual Reality or VR

Computer-created environment which closely imitates the real world in terms of effects used: it is three-dimensional, it is immersive, it allows things to be picked up and dropped, it gives haptic feedback. For some applications, a special helmet is needed with a display attached to the eyes, to "disconnect" from the real world.

VRML or Virtual Reality Modeling Language

The equivalent to HTML for 3D worlds. With VRML (spoken "vur'mel") objects can be placed in a virtual room, including mapped images, animation and sound playback. To view VRML files, a plug-in is needed that now often comes with web browsers.

WAV/AIFF/AU,GIF/JPEG/PNG,AVI/MPEG/Quicktime

Commonly used acronyms for common data formats used on the WWW. WAV, AIFF and AU are audio formats. GIF, JPEG and PNG are graphical formats to transmit images. AVI, MPEG and QUICKTIME contain movies and animations.

WWW or World Wide Web or The Web

One of the services offered by the Internet. The WWW is a global publishing medium for texts, audio and video. It is organized into single documents called pages. A WWW browser is needed to look at WWW pages.

Web addresses

DIGITAL CAAD BOOKS:
"Architektur mit dem Computer," Gerhard Schmitt, 1996: http://caad.arch.ethz.ch/projects/acm
"City of Bits," William Mitchell, 1995: http://mitpress.mit.edu/e-books/City_of_Bits/

ARCHITECTURE SCHOOLS:
Architecture ETH Zürich: http://www.arch.ethz.ch
Architecture Harvard University: http://www.gsd.harvard.edu
Architecture Columbia University: http://www.arch.columbia.edu/
Architecture Massachusetts Institute of Technology, MIT: http://alberti.mit.edu/ap/ap.html

ORGANIZATIONS:
Education of Computer Aided Architectural Design in Europe: http://info.tuwien.ac.at/ecaade/
The Association for Computer Aided Design In Architecture – ACADIA: http://www.clr.toronto.edu/ORG/ACADIA/home.html
American Institute of Architects (AIA): http://www.aia.org
International Association for Bridge and Structural Engineering (IABSE): http://www.iabse.ethz.ch/default.html
Swiss Computer Graphics Association: http://www.scga.ch

VIRTUAL MUSEUMS:
Virtual Palladio Museum: http://www.andrea.gsd.harvard.edu/palladio/museum.htm
Virtual chair museum: http://caad.arch.ethz.ch/teaching/nds/schreg/
Virtual Architectural Library: http://www.clr.toronto.edu:1080/VIRTUAL-LIB/arch.html
The World Virtual University: http://www.ccon.org/theU/index.html

BUILDING SITES WITH CAMERAS:
Berlin Potsdamer Platz und Spreebogen: http://www.icf.de/documents/cityscope/
Chemiegebäude ETH Hönggerberg: http://caad.arch.ethz.ch/projects/hci/Tracker/

CAAD RESEARCH
CAAD Futures 97 in München: http://www.arch.tu-muenchen.de/caad/cf97/
ACADIA 1997 in Cincinnati: http://www.daap.uc.edu/acadia/acadia97.html
CAADRIA 1998 in Osaka: http://caadria98.env.eng.osaka-u.ac.jp/

90

Scientific visualization http://www.inf.ethz.ch/department/IS/cg/html/agvis.html
Research CAAD ETH Zürich: http://caad.arch.ethz.ch/research/
Alter Ego Projekt: http://caad.arch.ethz.ch/RESEARCH/Alter_Ego
Information and Communication System: http://spp-ics.snf.ch/SPP-ICS/home.html
Case-based reasoning: http://caad.arch.ethz.ch/research/NFP-CBR.html
Sculptor: http://caad.arch.ethz.ch/~kurmann/*sculptor*/short.html
Building diagnostics: Center for Building Performance and Diagnostics
(CBPD), Carnegie Mellon University in Pittsburgh, Pennsylvania: http://www.
arc.cmu.edu/cbpd/

INTEGRATED PLANNING
CIFE project at Stanford University: http://www-leland.stanford.edu/group/CIFE/
The European COMBINE-Projekt: http://erg.ucd.ie/combine.html
SEED project at Carnegie Mellon University: http://seed.edrc.cmu.edu/
USA CERL in Urbana Champaign: http://www.cecer.army.mil/
ZIP Bau at ETH :http://caad.arch.ethz.ch/~buschm/zipbau.html

FACILITY MANAGEMENT
Center for Integrated Facility Engineering/ Stanford University: http://www-
leland.stanford.edu/group/CIFE/index.html
International Facility Management Association (IFMA): http://www.qns.com/
~okcifma/ifma.htm
Technical Research Centre of Finland (VTT): http://www.vtt.fi/

COMPUTER-SUPPORTED COLLABORATIVE WORK (CSCW) IN TEACHING
Hong Kong, Zürich, Seattle, Delft: *Multiplying time*: http://space.arch.ethz
.ch/VDS_97/
ETH Zürich, National University of Singapore: http://caad.arch.ethz.ch/
CAAD/sw94/sw94.html
ETH Zürich, University of Toronto: http://caad.arch.ethz.ch/CAAD/studio-
ca/studio-ca.html
ETH Zürich, MIT, Cornell, British Columbia, Sidney and Singapore: http://
caad.arch.ethz.ch/CAAD/studio-v95/vds95.html

VIRTUAL DESIGN STUDIO 1995 AT MIT:
http://web.mit.edu/afs/athena.mit.edu/course/4/4.156/www/Text/index.html

NEW FORMS OF TEACHING CAAD
CAAD Principia - Phase(X): http://space.arch.ethz.ch/ws97/
CAAD Design - fake.space: http://space.arch.ethz.ch/
CAAD 1. Semester - Informationslandschaft: http://alterego.arch.ethz.ch/infor-
mationslandschaft

CAAD 3. Semester - Raumgeschichten: http://alterego.arch.ethz.ch/ raum-geschichten

OUTSTANDING CAAD PROJECTS:
General: http://caad.arch.ethz.ch/teaching/wfp/
Max Bill and his work: http://caad.arch.ethz.ch/teaching/wfp/ ABGESCHLOSSENE/mathis/
Building cost simulation – Home Invest: http://caad.arch.ethz.ch/ teaching/wfp/ABGESCHLOSSENE/staeger/
Reconstruction of the Villa Poiana by Andrea Palladio: http://caad.arch. ethz.ch/teaching/wfp/ABGESCHLOSSENE/schaerer/
Weissenhofsiedlung in Stuttgart: http://caad.arch.ethz.ch/teaching/ wfp/ABGESCHLOSSENE/lindner/
Mies van der Rohe and the Mountain House: http://caad.arch.ethz.ch/teaching /wfp/ABGESCHLOSSENE/vonwil/
Aquamicans by Fabio Gramazio: http://caad.arch.ethz.ch/projects/aquamicans/
Architecture & Media: http://caad.arch.ethz.ch/~patrick/LOCAL/ projects/ss/index.html
Spatial quality of computer images: http://caad.arch.ethz.ch/teaching/ wfp/ABGESCHLOSSENE/felix

ARCHITECTURE IN THE INFORMATION SPACE
Archeology of the Future City: http://caad.arch.ethz.ch/trace
Digital city Berlin: http://www.is.in-berlin.de oder http://www.chemie.fu-berlin.de/BIW/d_berlin-info.html
Digital city Delft: http://www.dsdelft.nl/~delft750/inhoud.html
Digital city Eindhoven: http://www.dse.iaehv.nl/
Digital city Frankfurt: http://www.inm.de/services/webdept.html
Digital city Telepolis: http://www.lrz-muenchen.de/~MLM/telepolis/
Babylon-S: http://caad.arch.ethz.ch/~wenz/babylon/babylon_s/city/
Hollow Planet: http://caad.arch.ethz.ch/projects/babylon

Bibliography

Baudrillard J., *Simulacres et simulation*, Editions Galilee, Paris 1985.
Boyer M. C., *Cyber Cities – Visual Perception in the Age of Electronic Communication*, Princeton Architectural Press, New York 1996, Cover.
Dave B., *Towards Distributed Computer-Aided Design Environments*, in: proceedings CAAD Futures 1995, National University of Singapore, Singapore 1995.

Dawkins R., *The Selfish Gene*, Oxford University Press, New York 1976.

Engeli M., *Agents – Enhanced Reality*, in: Schmitt G., Architektur mit dem Computer, Vieweg Verlag, Wiesbaden 1996, pp. 110-111.

Faltings B., Hua K., Schmitt G., Shih S., Smith I., Bailey S., *Case-based Representation of Design Knowledge*, in: proceedings 1991 Defense Advanced Research Projects Agency, Workshop on Case-Based Reasoning, Washington D. C. 1991.

Frazer J. H., *An Evolutionary Architecture*, Architectural Association, London 1995.

Fünfschilling L., Schmitt G., *New Realities - Unterwegs zu neuen Realitäten*, Edition Museum für Gestaltung Zürich, Schweizerischer Werkbund, Zürich 1992, pp. 103-110.

Gero, J. S., Maher, M.-L. (Eds.), *Modeling Creativity and Knowledge-Based Creative Design*, Lawrence Erlbaum, Hillsdale, New Jersey 1993, pp. 354.

Hammond K., *Case-based Planning – Viewing Planning as a Memory Task*, Academic Press, Boston 1989.

Hirschberg U., Streilein A., *CAAD meets Digital Photogrammetry: Modeling Weak Forms for Computer Measurement*, in: proceedings ACADIA '95, Seattle, WA 1995, pp. 299-313.

Korth H. F., Silberschatz A., *Database System Concepts*, 2nd edition, McGraw Hill, New York 1991.

Kurmann D., Elte N., Engeli M., *Real-Time Modeling with Architectural Space*, in: Junge R. (Ed.), CAAD Futures 1997, Kluwer Academic Publishers, Dordrecht 1997, pp. 809-819.

Lashkari Y., Metral M., Maes P., *Collaborative Interface Agents*, MIT Media Laboratory, Accepted at AAAI '94, Cambridge 1994. http://agents.www.media.mit.edu/groups/agents/papers/aaai-ymp/aaai.html.

Madrazo L., *Typen & Variationen – Types & Instances (T&I)*, in: Schmitt G., Architektur mit dem Computer, Vieweg Verlag, Wiesbaden, 1996, pp. 126-127.

Madrazo L., *The Concept of Type in Architecture – An Inquiry into the Nature of Architectural Form*, Diss. ETH No. 11115, ETH Zürich, 1995.

McCullough M., *Abstracting Craft – The Practiced Digital Hand*, MIT Press, Cambridge, Massachusetts 1997.

Mitchell W. J., *City of Bits*, MIT Press, Cambridge, Massachusetts, 1995.

Mitchell W. J., *Computer-Aided Architectural Design*, Van Nostrand Reinhold, New York 1977.

MOCA, *The Archaeology of the Future City*, Exhibition Catalogue, Museum of Contemporary Art, Tokyo 1996, pp. 219-236.

Oechslin W., *Computus et Historia*, in: Schmitt G., Architectura et Machina, Vieweg, Wiesbaden 1993, pp. 14-23.

Roussel R., *Locus Solus*, Suhrkamp Verlag, Frankfurt am Main 1989.

Sanders K., *The Digital Architect, a Common Sense Guide to Using Computing Technology in Design Practice*, John Wiley & Sons, Inc., New York 1996, pp. 315-354.

Schank R. C., *Dynamic Memory: A Theory of Learning in Computers and People*, Cambridge University Press, Cambridge, Massachusetts 1982.

Schmitt G., *Architectura et Machina*, Vieweg Verlag, Wiesbaden 1993.

Schmitt G., *Architektur mit dem Computer*, Vieweg Verlag, Wiesbaden 1996a.

Schmitt G., *Design Assistants: Smart Objects and Personal Agents*, in: proceedings Descriptive Models of Design Conference, Taskisla, Istanbul 1996b.

Schmitt G., Dave B., Case-Based Architectural Design, The Experience of CADRE. Issues and Applications of Case-Based Reasoning to Design, Maher M.-L., Pu P., (Eds.), Lawrence Erlbaum, 1996b.

Schmitt G., *Design Medium – Design Object*, in: Junge R. (Ed.), CAAD Futures 1997, Kluwer Academic Publishers, Dordrecht 1997, pp. 3-13.

Schmitt G., Wenz F., Kurmann D., van der Mark E., *Toward Virtual Reality in Architecture*: Concepts and Scenarios from the Architectural Space Laboratory, in: Presence Magazine, Massachusetts Institute of Technology, Vol. 4, Nr. 3, Cambridge 1995, pp. 267-285.

Smith I., *Model-Based Design using Intelligent Objects*, in: proceedings Closing Conference Priority Programme Informatics Research, Jean-Michel Grossenbacher (Ed.), Swiss National Science Foundation 1996, pp. 69-70.

Stoll C., *Die Wüste Internet - Geisterfahrten auf der Datenautobahn*, S. Fischer Verlag, Frankfurt am Main 1995.

Streich B., Weissgerber W., *Computergestützter Architekturmodellbau*, Birkhäuser, Basel 1996.

Sutherland I., *Sketchpad, A Man-Machine Graphical Communication System*, in: proceedings 1963 Spring Joint Computer Conference AFIPS, Vol. 23, 1963.

von Buschmann D., Dave B., *Einsatz von Datenbank Systemen im Bauwesen, Teil 4*, Schlussbericht Integrierte Planung und Kommunikation im Bauprozess, KWF Projekt Nr. 2416.1, Professur für Architektur und CAAD, ETH Zürich 1995.

Wenz, F., Gramazio F., *Archaeology of the Future City: TRACE*, in: Schmitt G., Architektur mit dem Computer, Vieweg Verlag, Wiesbaden 1996, pp. 177-179.

World Commission on Environment and Development WCED, Oxford University Press, Oxford 1987, p. 46.

in Architecture
Series edited by **Antonino Saggio**

The Information Technology Revolution in Architecture is a new series reflecting on the effects the virtual dimension is having on architects and architecture in general. Each volume will examine a single topic, highlighting the essential aspects and exploring their relevance for the architects of today.

Other titles in this series:

Digital Eisenman
An Office of the Electronic Era
Luca Galofaro
96 pages, 60 color and 80 b/w illustrations
ISBN 3-7643-6094-1

HyperArchitecture
Spaces in the Electronic Age
Luigi Prestinenza Puglisi
96 pages, 60 color and 80 b/w illustrations
ISBN 3-7643-6093-3

Further titles will be published in the near future.

For our free catalog please contact:

Birkhäuser – Publishers for Architecture
P. O. Box 133, CH 4010 Basel, Switzerland
Tel. ++41-(0)61-205 07 07; Fax ++41-(0)61-205 07 92
e-mail: sales@birkhauser.ch
http://www.birkhauser.ch